Thomas J. Potter

Percy Grange

The ocean of life

Thomas J. Potter

Percy Grange
The ocean of life

ISBN/EAN: 9783741133930

Manufactured in Europe, USA, Canada, Australia, Japa

Cover: Foto ©Andreas Hilbeck / pixelio.de

Manufactured and distributed by brebook publishing software (www.brebook.com)

Thomas J. Potter

Percy Grange

PERCY GRANGE;

OR,

THE OCEAN OF LIFE.

A Tale, in Three Books.

BY
REV. THOMAS J. POTTER,
ALL HALLOWS' COLLEGE, DUBLIN,

AUTHOR OF "THE TWO VICTORIES," "LEGENDS, LYRICS, AND HYMNS,"
"THE RECTOR'S DAUGHTER," "LIGHT AND SHADE,"
"ST. PATRICK, A PANEGYRIC,"
ETC., ETC.

"A faithful friend is a strong defence; and he that hath found him, hath found a treasure." . . . . .
"A brother that is helped by his brother, is like a strong city."

Second Edition.

DUBLIN:
JAMES DUFFY, 15, WELLINGTON-QUAY,
AND
22, PATERNOSTER-ROW, LONDON.
1865.

TO

THE RIGHT REVEREND THE BISHOP,
THE CHAPTER,

AND

THE VERY REV. AND REV. THE CLERGY

OF

THE DIOCESE OF BEVERLEY,

This Work,

ONE OF A SERIES ILLUSTRATIVE OF PASSING EVENTS,

AND

OF THE PRACTICAL INFLUENCE OF RELIGION AND TRUTH

UPON DAILY LIFE,

WITH ITS TRIALS AND ITS TRIUMPHS,

Is inscribed,

WITH

EVERY SENTIMENT OF AFFECTIONATE VENERATION,

OF RESPECTFUL ESTEEM,

AND BROTHERLY LOVE.

CHRISTMAS, 1864.

CONTENTS.

	PAGE.
PREFACE, ...	vii

BOOK FIRST.

THE MOVING OF THE WATERS.

CHAP.		
I.	ATHERBY, ...	3
II.	"RED-NECKS,"	28
III.	PERCY GRANGE, ...	55
IV.	ILLUSIONS AND DIGRESSIONS, . . .	81
V.	THE "NATURAL MAN,"	93
VI.	THE MOVING OF THE WATERS, . . .	107
VII.	ON THE BRINK, ...	129

BOOK SECOND.

IN THE DEPTHS.

VIII.	DE PROFUNDIS, ...	179
IX.	DARKENING CLOUDS, ...	198
X.	A MOTHER'S LOVE—FAITHFUL EVERMORE, .	211
XI.	THE BURSTING OF THE STORM, . . .	226
XII.	FACE TO FACE, ...	246

CONTENTS.

BOOK THIRD.

BEATING TO THE SHORE.

CHAP.		PAGE.
XIII.	BEATING TO THE SHORE,	255
XIV.	LIGHT UPON THE WATERS,	265
XV.	COMING RIGHT,	279
XVI.	BEYOND THE EVERLASTING SHORES,	297
XVII.	CONCLUSION,	316

PREFACE.

I THINK that there is nothing to be said by way of preface to this book except that it forms the fifth volume of a series intended for innocent and rational amusement. In the introduction to "The Two Victories," the first of that series, I stated that I proposed to myself to illustrate and bring home to my readers, through the medium of amusing tales, those great events which are daily passing around us, events as important as they are interesting, but whose importance is, perhaps, scarcely realized in its full measure from the very fact that they are either comparatively little known, or appreciated as they deserve.

In furtherance of this project (without any undue attempt at preaching, without any design of writing a "religious novel," properly so called,) I have, in each of the volumes of this series, endeavoured to portray some one or other of the varied ways in which the grace of God acts upon the hearts of men in these our days, in leading them into the safe and pleasant places of his holy Church. The divine truth that the Spirit of God breatheth where He wills has never been more fully and more wonderfully verified than in the great religious movement of the last few years. Whilst each of my tales is the story of a conversion in some shape or other, I feel certain that, in no one of them, have I gone beyond what all my readers who have any experience on this matter will confess to be the limits of probability. I will go further, and say for myself that I have not gone beyond *facts*. I may have done my best to dress my story in an attractive shape. I am free to confess that I have laboured, honestly and earnestly, and with all the ability which I possessed, to tell that story as pleasantly as I was able, to surround it with all the interest which I could command; but, having granted all this, I will return whence I started, and repeat that my stories are substantially founded on facts, those facts which are continually taking place round about us, those facts which seemed to me as admirably adapted to form the basis of true Catholic tales, as, I am quite sure, they are worthy of being brought as widely as possible under the notice of the public. To bring, then, these great facts home to the minds and hearts of my readers, and to show them the working and practical influence of faith and of truth upon daily life, with its trials and its triumphs; to persuade them that the paths of love and of duty are those which can alone lead to happiness, even in this world, was the great object which I proposed to myself in this series. The undertaking was, in some measure, a bold one. In regard to the manner in which it has been carried out, I may say no more than that I have laboured to the best of my ability, in such leisure time as I have been able to snatch from other duties, to perfect and realize that which I began with a great earnestness and sincerity of purpose, with a real love for my work, and, above all, with a deep conviction of the necessity and the utility of every undertaking which promoted, no matter in how humble a degree, the diffusion of wholesome and sound Catholic literature. Less than this I could not honestly say. The success, I think I may say the *great* success, which has crowned my effort has proved that, at least, it was worth the making. If I could gain a higher reward than I have already received, it would be the thought that my success had encouraged others, possessed of higher abilities, and with more leisure time at their disposal, to devote them with as much good will as, I can say for myself, that I have done, to the same holy cause, the cause of our faith and the promotion of our literature.

Whilst my tales, certainly, do not profess to be "religious novels" in the ordinary sense of the word, it must be equally evident, from the idea which I have just given of their scope and their object, that they can have nothing in common with the "sensation" stories of the present day, even supposing that I could write in that style, which I cannot do.

I think it not improbable that some fault may be found with this story of "Percy Grange." I dare say some will assert that the character of the hero, if I may so call him, is overdrawn. I can only answer that, whilst I grant that the world, unfortunately for itself, does not possess such characters in very great abundance, I am equally certain that it does hold some such men as him whose character I have endeavoured to sketch in these pages. I am sure that such men are the light of the world, that they go far to redeem it from the littleness and the grovelling meanness which are its prevailing characteristics in these later days, that they are its glory and its exaltation. Although we may be compelled to confess, in sorrow, that we seldom come across such men, I think, when we do meet with them, that it is quite worth while to endeavour to bring their noble, if, perchance, their rare qualities before their fellow men; and, hence, entertaining this belief, I have not hesitated to make the principal interest of this story turn upon one against whom the objection to which I have alluded will, probably, be brought. Without asserting that I have professed to sketch a real personage, I will merely say that it has been my privilege to know, at least one, who more than realized every noble trait which I have endeavoured to paint in the hero of this narrative.

It may, perhaps, be also objected that the subject of my tale is of too serious, and even painful, a nature. I will only answer that life may be very peaceful and very happy, although it may be cast more amongst the realities and the shadows of our pilgrimage, than amid its sunshine and its flowers. But, I think that a man will, as I am sure he ought, write of life as he finds it. If a large portion of its realities, even of its sorrows, if you will, shall have fallen to his share, or have come under his observation, he will naturally write of life from that point of view. It may not be the most pleasant view of things, but, I am by no means sure that it is not the most useful. Even as I write, a certain solemn truth, which none may gainsay, is ringing in my ears, "That it is better to go to the house of mourning than to the house of feasting." Besides, it is well for us ever to remember that our sorrows come to us from the same beneficent hand which gives us our consolations and our joys—that the wind is ever tempered to the shorn lamb—that the great object of life is not pleasure, but duty—duty to God, and to our fellow men. It is well for us to remember this,—better still, to remember with a never-wavering hope that, if, on the ocean of life, we do but discharge our duty like earnest, simple-hearted men, taking the evil with the good, and the storm with the sunshine, although sorrow may endure for a night, joy shall surely come in the morning, shall come in that profusion which flows but from one hand alone, and that the hand of Him who sends us pleasure or pain as seemeth best to His infinite wisdom, the hand of Him whose mercies are above all His works.

> "All is of God! If He but wave His hand,
> The mists collect, the rains fall thick and loud;
> Till, with a smile of light on sea and land,
> Lo! He looks back from the departing cloud."

T. J. P.

Christmas, 1864.

BOOK FIRST.

THE MOVING OF THE WATERS.

" Lives of great men all remind us
   We can make our lives sublime,
And, departing, leave behind us
   Footprints on the sands of time;

Footprints, that perhaps another,
   Sailing o'er life's solemn main,
A forlorn and shipwrecked brother,
   Seeing, shall take heart again."

PERCY GRANGE,

&c. &c.

CHAPTER I.

ATHERBY.

FROM the inspired penman who tells us that man lives but a short time, and, living, is filled with many miseries—that he cometh forth like a flower and is destroyed—that he fleeth like a shadow, and never continueth in the same state—down to one, who, in our time has written, that—

> "Still on it creeps,
> Each little moment at another's heels,
> Till hours, days, years, and ages are made up
> Of such small parts as these, and men look back,
> Worn and bewildered, wond'ring how it is,"

how many wise, how many touching, how many stirring and but too true sentences have been penned regarding the shortness of man's life upon earth, and the mutability of all human things! Many of us, perhaps, have scarcely reached that somewhat indefinite period known as the prime of life; and, yet, where are the friends of our early days; where are those who sat on the same bench with us at school, who studied their Virgil or Cicero in the same class with ourselves, who shared in all our boyish diversions, and who, so far as man could judge, seemed to have as strong a grip upon life as ourselves? Alas, for the old, old story! The flower has been destroyed, and the shadow has flitted by; the silver thread has been broken, and the golden fillet has been rent in twain. We, ourselves, are still plodding on with weary, and, it may be, with faltering steps; now up and now down; and, spite of all our efforts, scarcely able to hold our own in the battle of life, till there are times enough when, were it God's good will, we could almost envy those who started in the race with ourselves, but who, beaten down and discomfited, broken utterly and hopelessly, have long since disappeared for ever from the course, but too glad to close their eyes upon the world, in the blessed hope of opening them again in that better land where there shall be no more hunger or thirst, no more suffering or pain, and where God, leading His children to the fountains of the waters of life, shall wipe away for evermore the tear of sorrow from the eyes which have wept their fill. When we were boys at school how glibly the old proverb used to run upon our tongue, *Tempora mutantur, et nos cum illis*, Times are changed, and we are changed with them; but it is only when year has followed year with such rapid succession that age is upon us almost before we had begun to think of its approaches, that we fully appreciate that times indeed are changed, and that we are changed with them. Not that I think there is anything in all this to make an honest, simple-hearted man melancholy or sad. There are times when my thoughts wander away to the past, and when the bygone years come before my mind so vividly that, for the moment, I seem to feel the earnest pressure of hands that have long since turned to dust, and to hear the sound of voices that long years ago spoke their last word upon earth; and, as I wake with a start from my reverie, I think that I should be less than a man if I did not find the tear trembling in my eye, if I did not find my heart beating somewhat more quickly than usual within my breast, if I could think without emotion of the graveyards where I saw true and faithful friends laid to their long, last rest. But such thoughts do not make me melancholy. God forbid. I suppose there are few of us who, at one time or another, have not lost a dear and faithful friend. But, if we were faithful to him in life, and if, at the last solemn moment, as we clasped his hand for the last time, and whispered into his ear our burning words of hope, of love, of trust eternal in the tender mercies of Him to whose bosom he was hastening, we also bade him remember that, as we had been faithful to him in life, as we were faithful to him in death, so, too, with a fidelity that should never swerve, with a loving remembrance that should never grow cold, would we be faithful to his memory for evermore,—I think there is nothing to make us sad or melancholy in the recollection of such a scene. Such scenes should but remind us of the day that is to come for ourselves. They should but stir us up to do our duty all the more earnestly, all the more honestly, all the more faithfully, in that state of life in which God's good providence has placed us; that so, when our brief span is exhausted, we may, in the trusting assurance of that duty faithfully and truly done, close our eyes upon a world that, at its best, was never more than a place of exile—that so, we may rejoin those whose fight was shorter than our own—those who were summoned to their rest and their reward long before ourselves. They should but remind us that time is passing onwards with its never-flagging steps—that every day the world is slipping more and more surely from beneath our feet—that every day which is added to the past does but make the inevitable end one day nearer for us all.

But, to put an end to these vague abstractions, which have been forced upon me, so to speak, by the task which I have undertaken in promising to pen the simple narrative which will form the subject of this book, I think, in all sober earnestness and reality, that nothing will so forcibly remind a man of the flight of time, and of the mutability of all human things, as a work such as that which I have entered upon in commencing this tale. You will, dear reader, understand more clearly what I mean, when I tell you that, at the very commencement, I must ask you to go back with me in imagination, I won't say to the *beginning* of the present century, but, at all events, to a period when it was still comparatively young. If, as a necessary consequence of such a request, it follows that I, the narrator of this history, am getting on in life, what can I do but confess the fact (I was going to say the melancholy fact, but I retract), and remind you that my gray hairs and my growing years may possibly be my misfortune, but that they, certainly, are not my fault, inasmuch as I am in no way responsible for them. Yes, I must ask you to go back with me a good many years, to the time when England was only just recovering from her long fears of Napoleon and the threatened French invasion, and when Waterloo was just as fresh in men's minds as Inkerman and Balaclava are in our own. I must ask you to accompany me (always in imagination) to one of the northern counties of England, let us say, Yorkshire. The time is five o'clock on a bright summer's afternoon, and the place is a quiet country village in the very heart of that rich and luxuriant county. The hay harvest is all over, and the reaping of the fields of waving corn has fairly commenced. Men, women, and children, are all out engaged on the work. None are left at home except the old and infirm, so that the village has quite a deserted look; and nothing breaks the stillness of the scene except that indescribable hum which sounds at once so soothingly and so pleasantly on a summer's afternoon, telling, as it does, of all nature at peace and rest, except, perhaps, the busy bee which flits so unceasingly about the flowers, and the varied insects which seem to find it almost too much trouble on this drowsy evening even to give out their usual hum or drone. Through the midst of the village there runs a small river, and all the cows of the parish, that can manage to make their way to it, are standing up to their knees in the stream, although they also seem almost too lazy to drive away, with a sweep of their long tails, the flies which torment them so unmercifully. Presently, the Rector and his wife drive by in a low carriage drawn by two handsome ponies. The Rector drives at a very leisurely pace, whilst his wife lounges comfortably at his side. A groom in a very smart livery sits in a little seat behind, bolt upright, and with his arms folded upon his breast. He looks decidedly ill at ease, and as if he would very much prefer to imitate the more comfortable position of his mistress, if the proprieties of life and the dignity of groomship would permit such an unheard-of innovation. The Rector (of whom we shall have more to say a little later) is a small, thin man, with gray hair, and with a pale and fretful, but, withal, intellectual face. He was educated for the bar, but the rectory of Atherby becoming vacant, and the presentation belonging to a member of his family who offered it to him, he forsook the bar, at which it must be confessed he had not attained a very high position, and entered the Church. When I have added that he is the younger son of an earl who was very glad to have him thus provided for, the rectory of Atherby being worth some two thousand a year, I have said all that is required in this place concerning him. The lady who lounges with such an aristocratic air at his side is a very different personage. She is very tall, and of commanding presence. Her large Roman nose tells of high breeding, whilst every gesture and movement show that she is one who is accustomed to move amongst the upper circles of society. However, like many another member of the upper ten thousand, her fortune was scarcely equal to her blood, and report says that she was glad enough to accept the Rector of Atherby when he made her an offer of his hand. It is not to be supposed that the high-born Rector and his aristocratic wife immure themselves the whole year round in such an out-of-the-way place as Atherby. The Rector has no such overstrained notions of duty as this would imply.

He deems that he has done all that can possibly be expected of him, when he has paid ninety pounds a-year to a curate, who has to undertake all the work of the parish, and maintain himself and family on this wretched stipend. Of course the Rector cannot help it, if the poor Curate is half-starved in his efforts to keep up the appearance of a gentleman on the income of an upper servant. The Rector only follows the ordinary custom, which he, surely, is not called upon to interfere with; moreover, does he not come down to Atherby in the autumn, when the London season is over, and assist in the work of the parish by preaching every second Sunday? Does he not distribute soup twice a week during the winter season, and how can he help it, if the people are so ungrateful as to stigmatize his charity as "dirty slop," and declare that it is made out of a sheep's head boiled in an unlimited quantity of water? The common people have always been proverbially ungrateful, at least so say the Rector and his wife, and they ought to know something about the matter. I am afraid that the gossips of Atherby are more than usually free with their tongues, as there is not one of them who is not ready to swear that the Rector's wife is a "Tartar," whatever that may mean, and that she leads the Rector a weary life of it. At all events, she contrives during the three or four months of their annual visit to Atherby to stir up against herself an amount of spite and ill-will which last the whole year through, and which find expression in a thousand acts of rancour and mischief. And yet, poor lady, perhaps she is scarcely to blame. It is not in the nature of things that she should understand the habits or the feelings of the humble folk who form her husband's flock; and hence, when she carries her aristocratic airs into their lowly cottages, and speaks to them with an hauteur which they bitterly resent, and with a shrinking and repugnance, not to say disgust, which she scarcely takes the trouble to conceal, she is, perchance, more to be pitied than to be blamed. It has never entered into her mind to conceive that the poor man is as proud and as independent in his own way as the king upon his throne; and, hence, if she grates against these feelings of the cottagers of Atherby till they scowl upon her with fierce and angry looks as she passes along the village street, and fasten the doors of their houses as they see her approach, she is certainly to be pitied almost as much as she is to be blamed. I dare say when she is whirling about in her well-appointed carriage through the streets of London she is quite at home; but when she comes down to Atherby, and tries to play the country Rector's wife, she is sadly out of place. It is one of the great mistakes of her life, a mistake all the more grievous because she does not perceive it. As I am introducing you, gentle reader, to Atherby for the first time, I am quite glad, for the credit of the village, that all the people are out in the fields as the Rector and his lady drive through the one straggling street, because you are thus spared the scowling looks and the angry expressions which I am afraid always greet their appearance. A moment more and they are out of sight, and the same drowsy stillness which was broken for a few minutes by their appearance has again settled upon the scene, but it is only for a second or two. Opposite the old village church stands a pile of ivy-covered buildings, which at once attracts the eye of the visitor by its quaint yet comfortable look. This is the famous Atherby school, and, as the church clock strikes the hour of five, the door of the school-room is thrown open, and the scholars come trooping out with a shout which rings through the quiet evening sky, and has such an effect on the cows in the stream below, that, with tails erect, they scamper off in all directions as fast as ever they can trot; so fast, indeed, that old Gaffer Oates who is hobbling by on two sticks opines that they'll do themselves a mischief, that they will; and causes the same old Gaffer, as he watches with evident anxiety and perturbation of mind, the antics and gyrations of his own particular beast, to exclaim more than once, "Drat them there boys, they're allas a-doing some mischief or other. If I'd my way, I'd mak'em shout to another tune, that I wad;" and as, at this juncture,

Gaffer Oates' cow, in the excitement of the moment, proceeds to make a furious and unprovoked assault upon an unoffending beast which is grazing peacefully on the river's brink, I am afraid the old gentleman's language becomes far too emphatic to bear repeating in the pages of a book like this.

But while Gaffer Oates is shaking his stick in impotent rage, now in the direction of his own light-minded and ill-conducted cow, and now in the direction whence the joyous shouts which have produced such an unexpected effect, are borne on the still summer air; ignorant and heedless of the old man's anger, the scholars of Atherby school are pressing in all the buoyancy of early youth through the old Norman arched doorway of the school-room, and spreading themselves in groups, according to their different tastes, through the large and level play-ground which runs down from the school-buildings to the public road, from which, however, it is cut off by a high wall and a couple of handsome iron gates. Just inside these gates there is a small lodge in which the porter resides. At the period of which I write, this office was held by a very cross-grained old fellow who had fought at Waterloo, and who, having left one of his legs on the field of battle, had been obliged to avail himself of the resources of science, which had supplied him with a limb of wood in place of that which he had sacrificed for the good of his country. I am afraid that we boys were far from appreciating as we ought old Peter's heroic efforts to keep us out of the clutches of the French; for, instead of looking upon his wooden leg with an eye of veneration, we were constantly casting it in his teeth, metaphorically, of course, in the shape of an opprobrious nickname, "Old Timber Toes," which was sometimes shouted through the playground till Peter was driven to the very verge of desperation. Between Peter and the schoolboys, therefore, the common state of affairs was one of war, subject, however, to truces of longer or shorter duration, as when Peter, being in more than ordinary good humour, would bring out a chair to the door of his lodge and tell us wonderful stories of the Peninsular war and the great battle of Waterloo. At these times Peter was in high favour, and as he never told a story without introducing Field Marshal the Duke of Wellington, and what the Duke said to him, Peter, on a certain memorable occasion, for the moment we looked upon Peter as a very great man indeed, and one who had been in intimate relations with the hero of the age. On this particular afternoon Peter seems to be in one of his worst humours, as he stands just inside his door, and watches the Atherby scholars forming into parties, according to the game in which they intend to take part. However, it is neither to Peter in his bad humour, nor to the seventy or eighty boys, of all ages and sizes, who are dispersed through the play-ground, that I wish to direct your attention, but to the three youths who have just issued from the school-room, and who are advancing, arm in arm, towards the iron gates. Both from their size and the respect with which the smaller boys make way for them to pass, you see at a glance that they are the seniors of the school. The one in the middle will, probably, arrest your gaze in the first place. The large, dark eyes, the magnificent, black, curling hair, the beautiful proportions of the neck, which is shown to advantage by the turn down collar and the loose blue tie, the aristocratic *pose* of the head, and the gracefulness and ease of every motion of his wellknit and handsome figure, combine to produce a form on which you will certainly look for a second time. His complexion is of a rich, deep brown, telling at once of robust health, and of constant participation in cricket, bathing, and all manly sports. As they advance towards the gates, at some remark made by one or other of his companions, he breaks out into a loud, hearty laugh, and as you look upon him, his face all mantling with pleasant smiles, and his teeth shining like two rows of pearls, I think you would have to travel many a mile ere you met a handsomer or more gallant-looking fellow than Tom Bowman. He is about eighteen, and has been at Atherby school for the last four years. He is the eldest son of a gentleman of good birth, who holds some high position or other in India, and it is said that Tom will be immensely rich. At present he has ten times as much pocket-money as any other boy in the school, and he spends it with all the liberality of a prince.

Whilst a more honourable and gentlemanly fellow than Tom was never born, you will, perhaps, not be much astonished to hear that he is at the head of all the fun and all the mischief carried on in Atherby school. No game of cricket in the summer, nor of foot-ball in the winter, could possibly be formed, unless Tom led one of the sides. If the village lads are to be engaged in combat, Tom must surely head the Atherby scholars to the field of war. Tom is a particular favourite with the smaller boys, for woe to him who dares to practise any act of oppression or injustice towards them; and many such an act has been nipped in the bud by the simple threat, "I'll tell Tom Bowman of you; and then you'll catch it, see if you don't." Tom was scarcely well out of one scrape before he was in another, and naturally enough he came in for a fair share of the punishments which were so liberally inflicted, according to the custom of these days, in Atherby school. However, he took it all as a matter of course, and would walk up for his flogging with as much coolness as he would take up his bat for his innings at cricket. I think the old Doctor, who was our head master, spared him as much as possible; for, spite of all his freaks and wildness, every one loved Tom Bowman. I never saw the Doctor thoroughly angry with him but twice, and it happened in this wise. One day, when we were taking our usual walk, one of the village lads brought a young jackdaw to Tom, and persuaded him to purchase it for a shilling. Tom secreted his bargain under his jacket, and so smuggled it into the playground; for it was one of the principal duties of old Peter to see that no contraband or forbidden articles were introduced within the gates. The next difficulty was, where the unfortunate jackdaw was to be lodged. After much deliberation and consultation Tom decided in favour of his desk. For a day or two all went on well enough, with the exception of a slight odour which proceeded from the desk, and which was not very pleasant to those who sat near. But on the morning of the third day the denouement came. Every morning, precisely at nine o'clock, the Doctor, who was a very pompous old man, came into the school-room in order to read prayers, which he did with a tone of voice and emphasis rarely heard in these days. I don't know whether Tom had forgotten to give the unfortunate bird his breakfast or not; but, at all events, as the Doctor was in the very middle of the prayers,

a loud *caw! caw!* resounded through the room.
Tom blushed to the roots of his hair, the boys
began to titter and cram their handkerchiefs into
their mouths to stifle unbecoming explosions, whilst
the Doctor, after one moment of silent indignation, proceeded with the prayers. He had scarcely
read three lines, however, before *caw! caw! caw!*
was repeated more hoarsely and more pertinaciously
than ever. It was no use this time. Heedless of
consequences, the whole school broke into one loud
roar, whilst the Doctor, hastily closing his book
and seizing his cane, came down from his pulpit,
and, waiving all further formalities, gave poor Tom
a most unmerciful flagellation. A few minutes
later old Peter stumped in, and pouncing upon the
poor jackdaw, wrung its neck with an amount of
hearty good will, which stung Tom a great deal more
than his flogging, and which laid the foundation
of a feud between them, which almost led in the
end to serious consequences. Peter had it in his
power to inflict many petty annoyances upon any
boy whom he particularly disliked, and he made
Tom feel the full force of his authority. Tom
bore it patiently enough for some time, and contented himself with plentiful and bitter allusions
to Peter's timber toes, whenever they happened to
meet. Having, however, received some more
than ordinary provocation, the nature of which I
forget at this lapse of time, he determined to
take ample revenge, and the plan he settled upon

was certainly as daring and ingenious in itself, as it was ignominious in the highest degree as regarded old Peter. Having first secured the co-operation of four of the senior boys upon whom he could rely, he unfolded to them the plan of operation, which was very simple. One autumn evening, Tom and his four associates contrived to absent themselves from the school-room, and about eight o'clock, when it was quite dark, crept down softly to Peter's lodge. Four of the party hid themselves behind a corner of the house, whilst the fifth, who had his face well muffled, so as to escape detection, knocked boldly at the door. Presently, old Peter made his appearance, grumbling and muttering, and evidently in the worst of tempers.

"Who's there, and what do you want?" muttered Peter.

"You're to go down to the school instantly," was the answer.

"It's no time of night to be sending for a poor lame man," retorted Peter, "and I won't go; no, I wouldn't go for Field Marshal the Duke of Wellington himself."

"You can please yourself about that," was the reply; "I have given you the message, and you can settle the rest with the Doctor. That's your affair and not mine. Good night;" and away went the pretended messenger and rejoined his friends behind the corner. They waited in much

anxiety for a few moments, to see how far the
spirit of rebellion and disobedience would prevail
over old Peter's notions of submission and dis-
cipline, and, in a short time, to their great joy,
they heard him sally forth. As he stumped past
the conspirators, "Now's the time," whispered
Tom, and, in a second, a large sack was thrown
over Peter's head, and fastened securely round
his waist. When he found himself thus caught in
a snare, he let off volley after volley of language,
much more forcible than correct or proper; but it
was of no avail. His arms were useless, on account of the sack in which they were confined;
and, as the battle of Waterloo had already disposed
of his legs, he was completely at the mercy of
his enemies. Without a word, but with all possible haste, they carried him back into his house,
and there, by the light of his own candle, thus
adding insult to injury, Tom produced a saw, and
deliberately sawed his wooden leg in two, a little
below where the knee would have been, if Peter
had possessed such a joint. The four held him pros-
trate, although, indeed, poor old fellow, it did not
require much force to keep him down, for, when
on his back, he was almost powerless, whilst Tom
operated in first-rate style upon the wooden leg,
and in a few minutes the work was complete.
They then untied the string of the sack, blew out
the candle, and long before old Peter could succeed
in disengaging himself, the conspirators were safely

out of the lodge, and had dropped, one at a time, into the school-room. Next morning, to the great astonishment of all except the conspirators, the bell did not ring at six o'clock to rouse us from our beds. The ringing of the bell was one of Peter's duties, and it was one in which he had never been known to fail. So surely as the first stroke of the church clock was heard, so surely, summer and winter, did the bell peal forth its unwelcome notice to the boys of Atherby school to be up and doing. However, on this particular morning, it was nearly seven before the bell was rung, and then evidently by an unpractised hand. A servant was despatched to the lodge to see what was amiss with Peter. He found that insulted and degraded veteran foaming with rage, and scarely able to tell the tale of his wrongs. The servant returned in a few minutes, bringing with him, for the Doctor's inspection, the portion of Peter's leg which had been sawed off, and an angry message from the veteran, to the effect that, if there was justice to be had in England, he would have it, or he would know the reason why. The story spread like wildfire through the school, and the moment breakfast was over the scholars rushed in a body down to the lodge, to get a glimpse of their enemy deprived of his leg. But the door was locked, and the curtains of the window closely drawn, so that their curiosity was doomed to remain unsatisfied. I think I never saw the Doctor so angry as he was that morning when he entered the school-room for first class. After a long and severe lecture on the unparalleled nature of the offence, he threatened to take such measures as would cause the whole school to feel the weight of his indignation, unless the author of the crime revealed himself, and confessed his fault. The words were scarcely spoken when Tom Bowman stepped out of his seat, and avowed himself the author of the crime. As he did so, with the half reckless, half defiant, but, above all, with the frank and gallant air which was so natural to him, a low murmur of applause, which not even the Doctor's presence could check, ran through the hall.

"I am the offender, Doctor," he said, "and I am ready to take my punishment."

"Who were your associates, sir," thundered the Doctor, "in this disgraceful act?"

"I cannot tell you, sir," answered Tom; "I alone am to blame, and I beg that I alone may bear the punishment."

"I insist upon knowing your companions," retorted the Doctor. "You were not alone in this infamous proceeding, and I will flog you within an inch of your life unless you reveal your accomplices."

Poor Tom turned two or three shades paler than usual as he heard the Doctor's threat, but the compressed lips and the knitted brow showed

that the desired revelation was about the last thing
in Tom's mind. The Doctor insisted, and Tom
as firmly declined to "peach," till matters
were becoming very serious. "You may flog
me, sir, till I die," was all that he said, as he
clenched his fists and knit his brow more deeply
than before, "but you'll never make me do a
mean thing, and it would be a mean thing to tell
when I alone am to blame." I don't know how
it might have ended, if the four accomplices, of
whom truth compels me to confess that a personage who will figure somewhat prominently in
this narrative was one, had not stepped out at
this juncture and admitted their share in the
affair. The Doctor forthwith proceeded to pass
judgment upon us. Our punishment included con-
finement to the school grounds for a month, several
other very disagreeable impositions, and a caning
such as was seldom administered, even in Atherby
school. As poor Tom had borne the lion's share
in the mad adventure which had brought this
punishment upon us, so, he had to take the lion's
share of the flogging, which he bore like a hero as
he was. It was, however, a much more difficult
matter to pacify old Peter. For several weeks he
held out with a pertinacity and determination
worthy of one who had fought at Waterloo, declaring that he would make no compromise, but
that "he would bring us before our betters," and
that he would "law" us to the last extremity. It

required all the Doctor's authority, coupled with
a peace offering in the shape of a five pound note,
to make old Peter capitulate at last. I think he
never fully forgave us, but, at all events, he was
much more careful not to interfere with us for
the future, and we were quite satisfied with having
obtained this result. From this slight sketch of
some of Tom's exploits you will have formed an
idea of his character, and it is now time that a
few words be devoted to the companions who are
advancing with him down the playground, and to
whom I ventured, courteous reader, to direct your
attention.

The youth on his right is about the same age
as himself, and, although his features are of a
very different type, he is scarcely less handsome,
and is perhaps, even more noble-looking than Tom
Bowman. Heavy masses of bright golden hair
bring out his high and intellectual forehead in
all its beautiful and striking development. His
complexion is wonderfully pure and clear, and
were it not for his aquiline nose, sharp and distinct
as if it were carved in marble, and the energy
and determination expressed in the somewhat small
but exquisitely-formed mouth, the large, full, blue
eyes would impart an air of languor, almost of in-
decision, to his face. As it is, they only serve to tone
down and soften the pride and haughty reserve
which, but for those redeeming eyes, would be the
prevailing expression of his features. Of much

slighter build than his companion, you see at once
that his inclinations will tend to study and intellectual, rather than more boisterous pursuits. When I
have told you that his name is Eustace Percy, and
that he is the second son of Sir Percy Percy, the representative of one of the oldest families in the
north of England, I have said all that is necessary about him in this place, always taking it for
granted, of course, that you understand that he is
one of the dearest fellows in the world; that he is
full of noble, chivalrous, and honourable feeling:
a worthy scion of a house that prides itself that
no blot can be found on its escutcheon, that no
stain can be fixed upon its unblemished name.
Although, perhaps, somewhat out of place, I will
add that, at the time of which I write, I think I
would willingly have laid down my life to serve
him, the dearest friend I had upon this earth.

The youth upon the left is the writer of this
present narrative, and as I cannot be expected to
give any description of myself, more especially at
this lapse of time, for you will remember I am
writing of a period when the century was comparatively young, I will merely say that "I am the
only son of my mother, and she is a widow." She
never writes to me without reminding me that I
am the light of her eyes, and the life of her heart;
and that if anything happened to me she should
never lift up her head again. I know that she
never rises in the morning, or retires to rest at

night, without imploring God, on her bended knees, to make her darling a good, a true, and honourable man. At the best I am but a thoughtless, heedless boy; but still, I never forget her poor pale face, her low, trembling voice, or the gentle motion of her hands, with which, when I am at home, she puts away my hair from my brow, that she may kiss it and press it to her own sad face. I never forget that soft, soft step with which she steals into my little room when she thinks I am asleep. I never forget how she kneels by the side of my bed and prays for me in the stillness of the night, prays until I pretend to wake with a sudden start, that I may open my eyes to look into hers the love which I cannot shape into words, and draw her face closer and closer to my own. I never forget how sparingly for many a weary year she has husbanded her scanty means, and pinched herself in a thousand ways that she may give me the education of a gentleman. No, thank God, I never forget these things, and the remembrance of them has kept me out of many a scrape, and made me overcome myself on many a drowsy afternoon, when the spirit of indolence was strong within me. As I have just said, at the best I am but a thoughtless, heedless boy, but, nevertheless, I have in all my vagaries and boyish failings at least one constant, never-changing resolution. It is, perchance, the only good that I have to say for myself, but never a day goes by that I do not kneel down, at least once, by the side of my bed, and beg of God, in my rough, boyish, and ill-connected words, that I may never add one tittle to *her* heavy load of sorrow and of care, that I may never cause one tear to flow in sorrow from her eye, that I may live to be the prop and stay of her declining years. I will say no more of myself except that my name is Ambrose ———, and that on this present summer afternoon I am something more than eighteen years of age, and the senior of Atherby school.

Having thus briefly introduced you to the three seniors of our school, who are to figure, more or less prominently in this narrative, I will only add that, although I have not the great worldly expectations of Tom Bowman, any more than I can claim the high birth of Eustace Percy, I believe in my heart of hearts, that, *positis ponendis*, as philosophers have it, you would have to travel a long distance ere, in this year of grace, 182—, you would find three stauncher, truer, or more faithful friends than the seniors of Atherby school, who, with a distant nod to old Peter, which he scarcely condescends to return, have just passed, arm in arm, through the iron gates which lead from the school to the village below.

CHAPTER II.

" RED-NECKS."

HAVING in the last chapter introduced myself and my two friends to you, it follows naturally that I should say a few words as to the origin of the aforesaid friendship. Eustace and I have been companions from our earliest years. My poor father was rector of the parish in which the old baronial hall of the Percys is situated, and from which the village takes its name, and I think he had been at college with Sir Percy, the present baronet. The living was not a rich one, and, when my father died suddenly, leaving my mother slenderly enough provided for, Sir Percy had been very kind to her in his own cold, haughty way. Although she was far too proud and independent to receive any pecuniary assistance at his hands, she had gladly accepted his offer, an offer made with all possible delicacy and good breeding, to allow me to avail myself of the services of the private tutor who attended his own sons. Hence, as soon as I was old enough, I used to go up to the Grange every day, and share in the lessons of Rupert and Eustace, the two sons of Sir Percy Percy.

I seldom saw Sir Percy, but, whenever I chanced to meet him, he always spoke kindly, if coldly, to me. It wasn't in his nature, I think, to speak warmly to any one. The tutor was an elderly, kind-hearted gentleman, who had, I fancy, been unfortunate in life. To me he was a real and true friend; and, if he made any distinction between myself and the sons of his patron, it was merely that he paid me more attention, and seemed more solicitous about the success of my studies. My mother was truly grateful to Sir Percy for his kindness, in thus affording me the chance of acquiring an education far above what her means would have allowed, whilst to me the advantages of such an opportunity were of the highest value. I had no other companions but Rupert and Eustace. I never took much to Rupert. Although he never threw into my teeth, as many boys would have done, the advantages which I was enjoying through the kindness and generosity of his father, he always contrived, somehow, to make me feel the difference in our position; whilst the coldness and reserve of his manner chilled me, and effectually prevented anything like intimacy between us. But with Eustace it was very different. We seemed to take to one another from the first. When we were too young to be more than mere childish playfellows we were most affectionate playfellows. As we grew up, the childish affection deepened into a true, earnest, never-wavering friendship. Unlike the generality of boys' friendships, which are so fickle and uncertain, ours never changed. He took the place of brother and sister to me, and divided the empire of my young and ardent love with her who was his only rival. I look back through the mists of many troubled years to those early days, and the coldness and the stern realities of the present seem to me to melt away and be lost in the remembrance of a friendship that was as pure as it was deep, as true as it was strong. I loved, with all my heart and soul, the noble, gentle-hearted boy who seemed to pour out upon me all the tender sympathies, and all the generous impulses of his fervent nature; who came to me in all his little griefs, and made me the confidant of all his boyish aspirations; who seemed to lean with such a frank and ever-trustful confidence on my will, a will, perchance, somewhat sterner and more rugged than his own. As I have just said, I loved him with all my heart and soul; with a love to which I can look back and say, in my heart of hearts, that the remembrance of it is coupled with no regrets, with no recollection which I could wish to be swept away and hidden from my sight. In the innocence of my early youth I opened to him all my heart, and with a simplicity and truth which admitted no less holy thought than that he was infinitely worthy of the best affections of my soul, I shrined him, once and for ever, in its love. I accepted, without shrinking, without one misgiving thought, the surrender of himself which he seemed to make to my stronger will. I accepted without hesitation that influence over him to which he seemed to invite me; but, although there were times when that influence was very strong, and when I was called upon to use it in very critical circumstances, I can lay my hand upon my heart, and thank my God in my inmost soul, that I never exerted it except for what I thought to be his good, except to make him, if that had been possible, a more noble, a more gallant, a more honourable, and true English gentleman. No matter what I myself might be, I would have died before I would have used my influence over him to lead Eustace Percy, even by one hair's breadth, from the path of duty and of right.

I pursued my studies in the manner already mentioned until I was about fourteen years of age. At this time Sir Percy determined to send Eustace to Atherby school, whence, in due season, he was to proceed to Oxford. Atherby school was partly endowed, that is to say, there were a number of free scholarships attached to it, and to one of these Sir Percy, by his influence, got me nominated. I had no hesitation in accepting the nomination; firstly, because, without it, an education such as that imparted at Atherby would have been altogether out of my reach; secondly, because my position would be in no wise different from that of the other pupils, as the names of the fortunate scholars were known to the authorities alone; and, thirdly and principally, because I should by this means still pursue my studies in company with Eustace, who, I need scarcely say, was not upon the " foundation." Although very undecided in my own mind as to my future profession, my poor mother had set her heart upon my entering the Church. I therefore went to Atherby with the intention of gaining, if possible, one of the " Exhibitions " belonging to the school. This exhibition, if I could succeed in gaining it, would entitle me to enter one of the colleges in Oxford, and would supply me with fifty pounds a-year for three years, a noble prize for a youth in my position. For this exhibition I had been studying hard for nearly four years previous to the time when I first introduced myself to your notice, and, at the ensuing Christmas, I was to stand my examination. If I succeeded, I should at once proceed to Oxford as an undergraduate. Whether *I* succeeded or not, Tom and Eustace were to enter Oxford as gentlemen-commoners the next term, a fact which exercised no little influence on my studies. To me, however, whilst it was a matter of life and death, as far as my future prospects were concerned, to them, success in their studies, either at Atherby, or later on at Oxford, was a matter of very minor importance.

The way in which the friendship between Tom

Bowman and me originated was so characteristic, that, with your leave, I will briefly narrate it. In the year 182—, boys were boys, and nothing more. They did not aspire to be men before their time—aping the manners and the dress, and I am afraid in too many cases, the vices of their elders. On the Sunday after my arrival at Atherby I had arrayed myself in a resplendent pair of white trousers, which were quite the fashion in those days, and of which, I dare say, I was vain enough. My vanity, however, was destined to receive a very unforeseen and mortifying check. When afternoon service was over, and I was strutting about the grounds, as proud as a peacock, Tom Bowman came over to me and invited me to inspect his garden. Suspecting nothing wrong, and proud to be noticed by Tom, I at once accepted the invitation. There was nothing particular in the little plot of ground which, by a considerable stretch of language, Tom called a garden, except a large stone, and some miserable-looking grass, diversified with, here and there, a plant of the very commonest kind. However, taking me by the arm, Tom invited me to enter and "look about me," as he expressed it. I thought he was hurrying me rather unnecessarily to the further side of his wretched grass-plot; but, in a second more, to my intense astonishment, I felt the ground suddenly give way beneath my feet, and when I recovered from my surprise, I found myself standing up to my knees in a hole full of mud, with Tom on the brink, laughing with all his might and main. I found afterwards it was one of his practical jokes to dig a big hole in his garden, fill it with mud, and then covering it so artfully with sticks and thin sods that it was almost imperceptible, lead some unsuspecting youth into it, as had happened to myself on this occasion. My first impulse was to cast a doleful glance at my white trousers, which were irreparably ruined; my second, to be revenged. Tom was always a good deal of a dandy in his dress, and on this Sunday afternoon, as I remember well, he was arrayed with more than usual smartness in some very gay, light-coloured clothes: so, whilst he was standing on the brink of his pit, laughing more loudly than ever at my mishap, I quietly stooped down and filled both my hands with his filthy mud, which, before he had time to think of what I was at, I discharged plump into his delicate-coloured vest, completely covering it, and imparting more than a sprinkling to his shirt-front and the rest of his garments. I shall never forget the look of astonishment which crossed his face at what, I suppose, he considered a very audacious act on my part. Still, even in the hurry of the moment, I could see that he admired my "pluck." However, he either was, or pretended to be, very angry, as he cried out to me:—

"I say, young fellow, you're coming it rather

strong, you are; but I'll teach you manners, never fear."

"I'll come it stronger, you treacherous scoundrel," I answered, "if you only wait till I get out of this confounded hole;" and out of it I scrambled as fast as I could. Tom saw what I was up to, and squared his fists to receive me. However, I had no intention of fighting a pitched battle with him, and so I ran in and closed with him at once. We were pretty fairly matched, and a tremendous tussle we had of it. However, wrestling was one of our Yorkshire games, and I saw in an instant that I had slightly the advantage of him. I think it was one of the toughest jobs I ever had in my life; but, at last, I got him to the side of the hole, and making one tremendous effort, I forced him over the edge, and as he clung to me with a grip like that of a vice, in we both went together. As soon as we were fairly at the bottom of the mud-hole, by a mutual impulse we unwound our arms, and looked each other in the face. I *felt* that I was very pale, and my breath came in short, hurried gasps; but I stood upon the defensive, not knowing what the next move on my adversary's part might be. He looked at me for a moment with a very curious expression, wiped away the sweat which was pouring down his face, and in a second more, broke out into one of his ringing laughs, as he held out both his hands to me.

"I say, old fellow," he cried, as he nearly

wrung my arm out of joint, "you're a plucky one, and no mistake; you and I ought to be great friends. What do you say?"

"With all my heart," I answered; "I bear you no ill will for this business; and, it strikes me, we're pretty nearly equal."

"Yes, I think we're about equal, old chap," he cried, more boisterously than ever; "but, give me your hand upon it once again, for, you know, you and I are to be great friends for the future."

I gave him my hand once more, and then we scrambled out of the hole as well as we could, presenting an appearance which would have brought as little credit to Atherby school, if any stranger had happened to see us, as it would have conduced to the Doctor's general equanimity of mind if he had chanced to come across us.

From that day forward Tom Bowman and I were true and staunch friends. Not that I mean to say that I put him in the same category with Eustace, or that I ever felt towards him in precisely the same manner that I did towards my earlier friend. I cannot exactly describe, and, perhaps, I had better not attempt to do it, the difference between my friendship for Tom and for Eustace; but there was a difference for all that, and a difference which I felt very clearly; although I might not be able to explain it. I would have made great sacrifices to oblige Tom; there was scarcely anything in honour and moderation that

I would not have done for his sake, but yet, I felt that, in his case, there was a limit to my self-sacrifice, a point beyond which I would not go; whilst I thought that my friendship for Eustace would stand any test. At all events, as I have just said, from the day of our tussle at the mud-hole to the hour when I laid his head back upon his pillow, and closed his bright, dark eyes in their long, last sleep, I was as true and faithful to Tom as he was ever frank, open, and true to me; and although there was a time when a dark cloud came between us for a while, I never loved him the less, I was never the less anxious for his weal, I was never the less ready to shut my eyes to what I did not wish to see in him, never the less ready to palliate and make excuses for what I was obliged, spite of myself, to behold, and, if I must speak the harsh word, condemn.

Of course Tom could not know me without knowing Eustace too, and during the four years we were at Atherby school we were almost inseparable. I say *almost* inseparable, because Eustace never took part in any of Tom's mad pranks. Tom would as little have thought of inviting Eustace to share in any of his adventures as I would have allowed him to do so. The gentle, shrinking, almost timid nature of Eustace withdrew him from anything like disorder or tumult. There was such an evident and palpable incongruity between riot, in any shape, and Eustace, that, heedless, unreflecting boys as we were, we should on the memorable occasion when Peter's artificial limb was sacrificed to our resentment, as soon have thought of inviting the Doctor himself as Eustace to join us in that exploit. No, he was the companion of our better and our purer moments. His very presence seemed, somehow, to soften us down, and to exert a mild and gentle influence upon us. We seemed to speak more guardedly and with more reserve when he was with us; and, I know for myself, that the rough jest and the thoughtless word were always repressed when Eustace was leaning on my arm, or speaking to me in his low and sympathetic voice. I speak of his voice as sympathetic, because I know no other word which will express what I mean, which will express that wonderful quality which his voice possessed of moving and of thrilling the souls of those who listened to him, as he spoke on subjects which excited either his pride or his enthusiasm. His soul was full of that exquisite sensibility, that keen appreciation of everything that is true, and noble, and great, which makes men, such as he, poets in the full sense of the word; and which, whilst thus filling their own hearts to utter overflowing with all that is beautiful and true, gives them such a wonderful hold upon those who have been cast in a mould rougher and less highly finished than their own. Eustace was too retiring and of too shy a nature often to " let himself out," as it is commonly expressed; but, when he did, when we got him into some subject to which his heart warmed, and which stirred the softer, but deep and sensitive chords of his enthusiastic nature, I asked in my boyish days no greater treat, no higher bliss, than to sit at his feet, and in loving silence look up into his kindling face, and watch his flashing eyes, as the burning words came pouring from his lips with a force which I neither could nor sought to withstand, with a power and depth which seemed to knit my whole being in a mysterious sympathy with his own. You will remember that I said some time ago that Eustace, as a general rule, leant upon my more rugged nature, and surrendered himself in a certain sense, to my guidance, seeming to invite me to exercise whatever influence I wished over him. But *his* influence over me was wonderful too; an influence which is almost as inexplicable to me now, as it was then; an influence for which I cannot account, except it be that truth and purity must always make themselves felt wherever they exist; and I know that Eustace was always both true and pure. In the midst of many temptations, in the midst of a moral atmosphere that was, God knows, murky enough, Eustace never lost any of the freshness and the innocent simplicity of his guileless nature. I did not know it then, but I know now, that God had great designs upon him; and so, as He brought the three children safe out of the midst of the fiery furnace, did He, by the exercise of the same omnipotent power, bring Eustace Percy safe and unscathed out of the perils and evil influences of a great public school, never ceasing to watch over him with the same paternal love and care, till He had purified and made him fit even for Himself.

We were in our last " half" at Atherby school when an event occurred which caused no small commotion in the parish, and which I have a special reason for mentioning in this place. From all that I have said, you, doubtless, have gathered that we were Protestant boys at a public Protestant school. At the time of which I write, the Catholics, or, as the members of the old faith were more generally called in our part of England, the " Papists," "Papishes," or " Red-necks," were, in the fullest sense of the word, "*raræ aves.*" So far as I ever heard, there wasn't even a solitary " Papist" in all Atherby. About four miles from the village, indeed, there was a quaint old house buried in a grove of trees, and the owner of it was said to be one of the proscribed race. He used sometimes to ride by our school, and I remember well his grave and venerable, but subdued, and depressed look. He was the representative of one of the oldest families in the county, one of those families who deem it their highest privilege, as in truth it is, to be able to say that they never " lost the faith." Spite, however, of his unblemished pedigree and his noble name, a name which shone conspicuously in the annals of the brightest days of his country, he was a lonely and a solitary man. Prejudice was far too strong in those days to allow the other county families, even the most mushroom-sprung amongst them, to associate with the "Papist;" and I remember how, on those rare occasions on which he rode past our gate, we used to gather in clusters around it, and watch him, almost as if he were some strange animal, until he was out of sight, whispering all the while our boyish stories about Guy Fawkes and the Gunpowder Plot, together with the other venerable and veracious traditions which we had inherited from our nurses and our grandmothers. I remember well his riding by one fifth of November, whilst we were enjoying our usual holiday in honor of that glorious festival, party feeling running very high amongst us at the time. We were engaged in manufacturing an immense "Guy" for the evening's bonfire, when it was whispered round that the Popish squire was passing, and away we all ran to the gates in order to see him. He was riding in his usual slow and depressed manner, his head bent a little forward on his breast, and his long, white hair falling down upon his shoulders. Although he had to pass close by the gates of our school, he never looked up, or took the least notice of us, till, incited, I suppose by the evil passions which had been stirred up in our breasts, we began to cry out

"Papist," and "Red-neck." It commenced almost in a whisper, but, in a moment, it rose to a fierce and angry cry, a cry all the more discordant and fiend-like, that it came from the lips of boys such as we were. I was standing in front of the gates, and as the evil sounds fell upon his ear, I saw that a deep and burning flush passed across his face. I marked his hand close with a nervous twitch upon his heavy riding-whip, and, as he reined up his horse with a sudden check, I expected for a moment to see him ride full upon us, and administer the punishment which we so richly deserved. A moment more, and the flush had passed away, to be succeeded by a deadly pallor, which, as I marked it, filled me, even at the time, with a feeling of sorrow for him, and a deep compunction for my own unworthy conduct, in thus insulting such a noble and a true gentlemen as it was evident he was. The same feeling made me resolve, as he struck his spurs into his horse and rode hastily away, that I would never again so far forget myself as I had done on this occasion. Nay, so sudden was this revulsion that, although I had been one of the first to raise the obnoxious cry, I remember I turned round and relieved my feelings by soundly boxing the ears of some half-dozen small boys, who were still yelling after the "Papist;" the aforesaid small boys expressing, both by word, and still more by looks, considerable astonishment and disgust at my flagrant and inexplicable inconsistency. However, I merely mention this incident to bring more clearly before my readers the position occupied by Catholics in the county of which I write in the year 182—, and that they may more fully understand the feelings of astonishment, of indignation, and even of alarm, which pervaded the breast of every man in the parish of Atherby, when, without any previous forewarning of what was coming, it was suddenly rumoured abroad that the eldest son of a neighbouring gentleman had " turned Papist."

This gentleman had been one of the firmest props of the Church, an earnest, stern, uncompromising Protestant; the last man in the world of whom you could have predicted that such an unheard-of event would take place in his family. Summer and winter, rain or fair, in every season, and in every weather, we had seen him, accompanied by his family, drive up to the church twice every Sunday, as regularly as the Sunday itself came round. He was always one of the first to enter his pew, and one of the last to leave it. The rector of Atherby didn't trouble himself about " monthly communion," and other new-fangled notions, which, even at this time, were beginning to make themselves known. He adhered to the good old practices, and thought that if he gave his flock (save the mark) the opportunity of " taking the sacrament" four times in the year, it was quite sufficient to satisfy their devotion (which, I dare

say, was true enough), and his own obligations.
In fact, the fervour and devotion of Atherby
had become so uncommonly cool and unexacting that, although at least four or five villages
were comprised in the parish, the communicants
never exceeded twenty, including the rector and
his curate, the parish clerk and the sexton, with
several other dignitaries and hangers-on to the
church by law and act of parliament established
amongst us, for purposes which may have been
very clear to the devisers of the aforesaid
acts of parliament, but which are not easily
fathomed by less acute or less enlightened intellects. Still, whenever the sacrament was administered, amongst the foremost and most devout of the communicants had always been this
good gentleman, and his eldest son, who, having
now attained his majority, had so suddenly
" turned Papist." I never heard the history of
this young man's conversion, or how it came to
pass; but I remember well the commotion which
the news of it caused in Atherby school, and, still
more, in Atherby village. I am quite sure that if
the Popish squire had dared to show his face at
this crisis of affairs, he would, at the very least,
have been hooted and pelted out of the place. The
rector was absent at the time, but he posted down
in hot haste, that he might be on the spot to
prevent the contagion from spreading, even supposing there had been any danger of such an

occurrence, and it was publicly announced that he would preach a sermon in connexion with recent events. I remember that sermon well, for there were various circumstances in connexion with it which impressed it deeply on my memory. First, there was the entrance into the church of the father of the unfortunate renegade. He had always borne the character of a harsh, stern man, a man who had been but little loved by his neighbours and acquaintances in his own sphere of life, whilst his severity as a magistrate had rendered him peculiarly obnoxious to the lower classes. All eyes were bent upon him as he entered the church on this occasion. It was only a fortnight since the report of his son's conversion had gone out, but, although he walked down the aisle to his pew with a step as firm as ever, and with a face which was perfectly cold and immovable in its stern severity, he looked at least ten years older. He had acted with true Protestant consistency, and had turned his son out of doors for daring to use his own judgment, even when salvation was at stake; but the settled gloom upon his face, the knitted brow, and the hair, which had turned so suddenly gray, told but too plainly how stern and relentless had been the fight, and how dearly the victory, such as it was, had been purchased. Although, as I have said, he was not a man whom many loved, nor a man who had ever been popular, I think there was no one in

Atherby church that Sunday who did not pity him from the bottom of his soul. For my part, I know that my heart softened towards him as it had never done before, and I felt as if I should have liked to have gone over to him, if I had dared, and take his hand, and tell him how much I sympathized with him in his heavy sorrow, and how I hated the vile Papists who had stolen his son away from him; and I am even afraid that if the Popish squire, to whom I have already alluded, had crossed my path at this time, I should once more have raised my voice against him, spite of the good resolutions which I made upon a former occasion.

In due season the rector ascended the pulpit. I was watching him very closely at the time, and it seemed to me that he cast a very anxious and perplexed look in the direction of the seat occupied by his wife. However, I had barely time to notice this, ere he commenced his discourse. I had often heard him preach before, but I had never heard a word bearing upon controversy drop from his lips. His ordinary sermons were certainly the very driest dissertations upon the most trite subjects; and his curate was a faithful imitator of his superior. But on this occasion we were evidently in for something very different. There was an unusual tremor in the rector's voice, and his face was very pale, as he commenced his discourse by remarking that recent events of a painful and very dreadful nature imposed upon him the obligation of warning his flock against the aggressions and the deadly cunning of the false and idolatrous Church of Rome. These words were scarcely out of his mouth when, to the intense astonishment of every one in the church, his wife rose from her seat and swept down the aisle with a step that would have become an empress, it was so haughty and defiant. Her lady's maid hurried after her; but, as she returned in a moment, it was evident that it was not indisposition which had caused the rector's wife to leave the church in this strange and abrupt manner. The rector turned paler still as his wife passed out of the church; but he quickly recovered himself and delivered his discourse—a discourse, the effect of which I can fairly say was very small, when compared to that produced by the inexplicable conduct of his wife. I need scarcely add that this event was the subject for a nine days' wonder to the villagers of Atherby, and one which caused the tongues of the village gossips to wag very freely. I never heard it explained. I know that the common impression was that the rector's wife had once been a Catholic, and had changed her religion when she married him. Others went so far as to insinuate that she had never changed her religion at all, but that she had merely given up the practice of it, being all the while a " Papist" in her heart. For her own sake I trust that there was no truth in these reports; but I am afraid they had some foundation. I am afraid she had sacrificed truth to interest, that she had bartered heaven for earth. Perchance, like other apostates, she had never lost her faith, and this faith had, spite of herself, risen up and asserted its dominion—had spoken to her with that voice which may be stifled for a time, but which can never be destroyed, and, working upon her strong will, and her naturally unbending disposition, had caused her to act as she did when her husband proceeded to vilify and traduce that religion which, no matter how she might have prevaricated from it, in her inmost heart she knew and believed to be the only true one. I am ignorant of her subsequent history, for she and the rector left Atherby the day after this famous sermon, and I left for good and all in the course of a few weeks, and before they had returned. If it were true that she was either an apostate or a woman who stifled truth and the dictates of her conscience for mere worldly motives, I hope and pray that she returned to the paths of duty and religion ere it was too late. I hope and pray that she went in humble sorrow and contrition to look for peace, and rest, and full forgiveness, where they could alone be found.

I have troubled my reader with these, perhaps, somewhat uninteresting details, because they contain the history of my first knowledge of, and acquaintance with, the Catholic religion. I may say that I had never heard of it before these events. Of course, I knew that there were a few people scattered here and there who were known as " Papists," and who were to be shunned by every one; for, in my young days, the word " Papist" was synonymous with idolatry, persecution, thumb-screws, visions of Guy Fawkes, and everything that was horrible. The events which I have related first brought this tabooed and dreaded religion home to me as a palpable and existent fact, and I need scarcely add, that the circumstances through which it was thus brought under my notice, were not of a nature to remove my prejudices, or render me more favourably disposed towards it I have also mentioned these things for another reason, which I will as briefly as possible relate to you.

As soon as the service was over on this memorable occasion, Tom Bowman, Eustace Percy, and myself began eagerly to discuss the events of the day. I don't intend to trouble you with an account of our sayings, which, doubtless, were more novel and wild than sapient. Whilst Eustace was inclined to side with the young man who had " turned Papist," and to hold that every one had a right to do as he liked in the matter of religion, I remember that I was very loud in my denunciations of Popery and everything connected with it; although I cannot remember that I brought forward any very solid arguments to support my

empty denunciations; in this respect imitating the
example of many eloquent orators (and especially
on religious mat ters) both of ancient and modern
times. Although I have just said that the three
of us began eagerly to discuss this matter, this is
scarcely correct, for I remarked that Tom was
unusually silent. Reticence, or backwardness in
giving his opinion, was not one of Tom's usual
failings; but, on this occasion, he said very little,
and that little was expressed in cautious, hesitating words, very different from his usual blunt
outspokenness. I remember that I was puzzled
at this; and, at last, after making some more than
usually offensive remark about the Papists, I ap-
pealed directly to Tom to support the opinions
which I had advanced. Fancy our astonishment
when Tom, blushing to the very roots of his hair,
not merely refused to add his testimony to mine
(on a matter of which I knew nothing), but absolutely went on to declare that he was half a
Papist himself, and that he would listen to no more
of my abuse of people of whom I was completely
ignorant. I saw Eustace give one great start as
the strange tidings fell upon his ear, and then he
took Tom's hand in both his own. For an instant
I felt a strong impulse to answer Tom in hot and
angry words, but I stifled my resentment, and took
his other hand in mine.

"Tom, my dear old fellow," I said, "I didn't
know of this, or else I would not have spoken as

I did. I didn't mean to offend you; indeed, I didn't; and, if I have annoyed you, I beg your pardon with all my heart," and I pressed his hand more warmly than ever.

Tom returned the hearty grasp of my hand, and I think I saw the tears come into his eyes, but, for a moment or two, he did not attempt to answer me. At length he led us over to a bench in a retired part of the grounds, and when we were seated under a tree, Tom began to speak to us in hot and impulsive words.

" I am sorry I have said so much," he said, " but I know that I can trust you, and so I will even say a little more. I know it's a shame for me to have kept this from you so long, because there ought to be no secrets between such friends as we are; but I didn't like to tell you, as I was afraid you mightn't think so well of me if you knew that I had any Popish blood in me," he continued, in a lower voice, and turning his head a little away from us, especially from me. However, I again took one of his hands in mine, and presently he went on. "Besides, you know," he said, half apologetically, "I'm not a Papist; I never said I was; but I'll tell you just how it is. My poor mother was a Catholic, and as long as she lived she brought me up in her own religion. She was the dearest mother in the world," continued poor Tom, big tears rolling down his cheeks the while; "and as long as she was alive my father never interfered with her, but allowed her to do as she wished with me. Soon after she died my father took his Indian appointment, and sent me to Atherby school. Before I came, he told me that I could do as I wished in regard to religion, but that, of course, he would like to have me believe as he did. I promised my mother before she died that I would never forget what she had taught me; but when I came here, and found that all the fellows were Protestants, you know, I was ashamed to say anything about being a 'Papist,' and so I have always gone to church with the rest of you, and I have almost forgotten everything that my mother taught me; and the end of it all is that I often think I have no religion at all now, and that it doesn't make any matter what I call myself. Only, Ambrose," he continued, almost fiercely, turning to me, "you know, I cannot stand hearing you talk in that way, and I believing it to be a foul lie. I know," he went on, his voice beginning to break, "that it would be a blessed thing for me if I could only be like my mother. I know that she was like an angel of God, and that she died when she did, because she was too good for the world, and God took her to Himself. I know that if God had left her to me I should have been a very different fellow from what I am. I know," he continued, between the great sobs which were now rising in his throat, "that I'm almost as bad as I can be. I know that I shall never come to anything good, and I know that my mother was as holy and as pure as ever she could be, and as long as I live I will never again allow any one to say that her religion was false or bad. I know you didn't mean it, Ambrose," he went on, turning to me again, " but it was a lie, it was a foul lie for all that; and, bad as I am myself, it is a lie which no man shall ever again repeat before me. For the sake of my dead mother I'll do that little at all events. God knows how faithfully I'll do that little," cried poor Tom, as at this point he fairly broke down, and, covering his face with his hands, wept aloud.

I think that Eustace and I each got hold of one of his hands, and I am sure that we did our best, our very best, to comfort and console him with such simple words as our affection and sympathy suggested to us in a plentiful abundance. The end of it was that Tom soon brightened up, and, after binding ourselves to guard his secret faithfully, we joined hands, and once more renewed a promise which we had already several times made to one another, viz., that, through all the trials and changes of the uncertain future that was looming on us, we would stand to each other with a faithful and a never-wavering friendship, with a fidelity which no possible change of circumstances should ever weaken, with a constancy which no cloud should ever darken or obscure.

In our ignorance of any harm, we confirmed

this promise with some solemn words, which I am sure we had no right to employ on such an occasion. How far this promise was rash, and with what degree of fidelity we who made it observed it, it is the object of this simple story to make known to the reader, whose patience may, perchance, have been somewhat tried by these introductory chapters—chapters, however, which were necessary for the due understanding of the narrative to be unfolded in the following pages.

CHAPTER III.

PERCY GRANGE.

THE events recorded in the preceding chapter took place in the autumn of our last year at Atherby; and at Christmas I stood my examination for the "Exhibition." It was, I think, about the hardest piece of work which I ever went through in my life; but my labours were crowned with success; and the flush of joy which passed across my poor mother's pale face, as she clasped me in her arms on my return home, more than repaid me for all my toil. Eustace and I travelled down to Percymoate together as soon as the school broke up for the Christmas holydays. As we were to return to Atherby no more, this breaking up had a more than ordinary significance for us. I suppose there are few boys who leave school for good and all without some feeling of pain. It is not possible, I think, to sever ruthlessly, and without some degree of sorrowful regret, all those associations which are wound up with the old schoolroom and the well-known seat, with the play-ground and its crowd of memories, with the village church, and, perhaps, the village house of entertainment for man and beast. Take it all in all, my days at Atherby school had been very happy and very peaceful; and it was with a feeling of true and deep regret that I went round for the last time to look at all the places in which I had carved my name; to take leave of all my friends and acquaintances; to say good-bye to scenes which, in all human probability, I should never see again. When I add that my heart even softened to old Peter, who had never looked half so good-natured or half so pleasant in my eyes as when I went to say a few kind words to him, and to beg his pardon for all past annoyances before I went away, you will not be surprised to hear that I fairly broke down as the Doctor held my hand for that last time, and begged of me in his own hearty, earnest words, ever to do my duty like a man; to be a comfort to my widowed mother, and a credit to Atherby school. After taking an affectionate farewell of Tom, who was to spend his vacation in London with a gentleman who was his guardian, and with many promises of frequent correspondence until we should meet again in Oxford, Eustace and I set off to Percymoate, the village in which my mother's little cottage was situated. The old baronial hall of the Percys is about three miles distant from this village, to which, as I have already said, it gives its name.

I was nearly nineteen at this time, and I have no doubt that I realized to the full the dignity of my position, now that my schoolboy days were over, and Oxford was open to me. As we travelled down home, I thought a good deal of the Doctor's last exhortation to me on parting, to do my best to be a comfort to my widowed mother, and a credit to Atherby school. I think I have already mentioned that my mother had set her heart upon my entering the Church of England; and although I had no great inclination for embracing that profession, still I had no great repugnance to it, and thought that it would do as well as anything else. I need hardly say that I regarded it in no higher light than as a very respectable means of earning my daily bread. I didn't know at the time how very hard so many unfortunate men find it to earn their bread, in the most literal sense of the word, in the aforesaid profession. I fancy that my thoughts were rather directed to those fortunate ones who have fallen into the possession of the loaves and fishes, than to the struggling curates, who have to strive to support themselves and their families, and to keep up a genteel appearance on a miserable ninety pounds a year. However, neither my thoughts nor my resolutions on the matter were very deep; but they all had one unvarying conclusion, viz., that I would stand to my mother like a man; that I would do my very best for her who had done and sacrificed so much for me; that I would make her remaining days upon earth as happy and as pleasant as never-failing love, and watchfulness, and care, could render them. As soon as the coach on which we had travelled turned into the street in which the village inn was situated, I caught sight of my mother's poor, pale face, which looked all the paler and more worn as she strained her eyes and gazed anxiously towards us, that she might catch the first glimpse of me. I waved my hand to her as we drove down the little street; and I scarcely waited for the coach to stop before I jumped off and got her in my arms. It was two years since I had seen her, and I think she was hardly prepared for the change in my appearance which had taken place during that period. I think I must have reminded her very forcibly and very painfully of him who had gone; for, after one long look into my face, in which she seemed to scan its every line and feature with a strangely sad and earnest scrutiny, she closed her arms tightly round my neck, and hiding her face upon my breast, sobbed and cried aloud; but I think her broken exclamations: "Oh, my darling; oh, my poor, poor darling," had almost as much reference to him whom she had lost, him whose memory she had cherished with such a true and faithful love, as to him whom she held in her arms and loved, as I knew well, more deeply and more truly than all the world beside. Although I was nearly nineteen and accustomed to look upon myself as almost a man, I am not in the least ashamed to confess, that

I drew her to me closer and more closely still, that I bent down my face, and pressed it to her own, and that I mingled my tears with hers. I remembered in my heart of hearts, not only then, whilst I held her in my arms, but also later on, whilst I was on my knees by the side of my bed, that I was the only son of my mother, and that she was a widow; and as I thought of this I knew that my tears were no disgrace to my early manhood. Before I laid me down to rest that night in the snug little chamber which I had always occupied, a chamber whose every arrangement seemed to speak to me of my mother's love and care, I once again called God to witness how truly and how faithfully I would guard and cherish her; and, when, after tapping at my door to know if she might enter, thus reminding me that she recognised the change in our relations, so to speak, which my advanced age supposed, for, formerly she had entered as a right without seeking for leave or permission, she came over to my bed and told me that she could not sleep without one more look at the darling of her heart, I put out my arms, and drew her face down to mine, and whispered in her ears the self-same words which I had spoken—the self-same promise which I had made to God but a few minutes before; and I thank that same God—oh! how I thank Him, that He enabled me to keep this promise, even in its lightest thought, to keep it in its fullest sense and hearing, to the latest moment of my mother's life.

On our arrival at Percymoate, a carriage from the Grange was waiting for Eustace. What was my astonishment when the servant approached and handed me a note, which I knew at once, from the coat of arms on the seal, to be from Sir Percy. The substance of its contents was a request that I would spend at least a fortnight of my vacation at the Grange. Sir Percy, however, added, that although I was to consider myself pledged to spend at least one fortnight with them, I was also to remember that this did not exclude my spending as much additional time with them as I could spare from my mother. In a postscript he added, that there was a pony in his stables which he would do himself the pleasure of sending down to our cottage next morning, and which, he trusted, I would consider at my disposal so long as I remained at Percymoate.

I don't know whether the contents of this note made my poor mother or myself the prouder, for, although, as I think I have already mentioned, Sir Percy had always been kind to me, in his own distant way, I had never been invited to stay at the Grange before. I felt both his kindness and his condescension (for, after all, there was a certain degree of condescension in his taking so much notice of *me*) very deeply. As soon as I could get away for a moment from my mother, I went over to Eustace, to make him acquainted with the contents of the note; and, from the flush which passed across his face, and the way in which he pressed my hand, I knew well how grateful he was to his father for this act of kindness towards me, and how deep and sincere was the pleasure which this matter afforded my dear friend, both on his own account and on mine. I charged him to bear my most grateful acknowledgments to Sir Percy, and then we parted for a time; but, as Eustace would have it, only till next day.

After spending a very happy and a very pleasant fortnight with my mother, I went to pay my visit at the Grange, a visit which I regarded as quite a great event in my life. Eustace came down to the village for me on the appointed day, and drove me to the Hall, which I confess that I entered with some little trepidation of spirit. Sir Percy received me very kindly, and assured me in words which, coming from him, seemed almost warm, that it gave him great pleasure to see the son of one of his earliest college friends under his roof. Although I lived to see him a poor, broken, miserable, old man, he was, at the time of which I write, as handsome and as noble-looking a gentleman as you would have found in all England. He was only a baronet, but he traced his pedigree up to a period when the names of many a family, which now rejoices in ducal honours, had never been heard of; and I firmly believe that Sir Percy considered himself as noble and as true a gentleman as the highest amongst them. If he were stiff and unbending to a degree that was hardly pleasant to those with whom he came in contact, you could not help feeling that this arose, not from any desire to make himself disagreeable, but simply from his overpowering conviction of his own dignity, and the grave responsibility that ever rested upon him, a responsibility of which he might not lose sight, even in his most unguarded moments, as the representative of a race, which counted I know not how many baronets of untarnished honour and of spotless fame in its line. Sir Percy kept very much aloof from the county politics. I dare say he shrunk too much from the contact with common people, which is the necessary fate of every one who ventures to take part in contested elections, and such like vulgar proceedings—and, although it was said that more than one government had shown very great anxiety to secure for itself the immense influence which he possessed as one of the largest landholders in the county, and had caused it to be made known to him that an earldom would not be considered as too high a reward for such services on his part, still, Sir Percy had never stirred. I am sure he considered that the blood of the Percys, which crimsoned his veins, could be ennobled by no title which any government could offer to him; and hence, although at election times he never failed to notify to his tenants, through his steward, his will that they should proceed in a body to vote for the Tory candidate, he never showed his patrician features on the hustings, or exposed himself to the risk of those unpleasant collisions with the mob which are so apt to rise in moments of excitement, and in which the same mob are equally apt to forget the respect and reverence due to their hereditary rulers. The only exception which I ever knew Sir Percy make to this rule occurred in this wise:— One election time, in addition to the legitimate contest between Whig and Tory which was always waged in Yorkshire, and for which the great rival families of the county supplied the candidates, the Radicals had the audacity to bring forward some low, manufacturing man or other in their interest, a proceeding, which, at that time, filled the aristocracy with mingled feelings of horror and disgust; for you must remember that I am writing of a period when the Reform Bill had not been passed, and when Radicals and radical principles were not so common as they are now-a-days. In order to mark as strongly as possible his disapprobation of such an audacious proceeding, Sir Percy, on this occasion, headed his tenants to the poll. I was only a boy at the time but I remember the sight well.

Sir Percy, stern and immovable, and looking neither to the right nor to the left, sat in an open

barouche drawn by four magnificent gray horses.
Blue streamers floated about their heads, whilst
the postillions and the two footmen wore rosettes
of the same colour on their breasts. Nay, Sir
Percy himself had so far conformed to the exigencies of the occasion as to wear a blue satin
cravat, and a blue rosette in his coat. Immediately
behind his carriage rode his tenants in large numbers, four abreast; stout, sturdy farmers, mounted
on steeds as sleek and comfortable as their masters.
As the procession passed through the village street
on its way to the county town, it made a gallant
show, and the low Radical, as was only right and to
be expected, was ignominiously defeated and put to
flight. Such, however, is the degeneracy of the
times, that I am afraid the old county families,
who so long looked upon its representation in the
senate of the country as belonging to them, quite
as a matter of right, find it hard enough to hold
their own now-a-days; when the Radical with
abundance of money at his command is just as
acceptable, if not more so, to the common people,
as the high-born gentleman, who, although all
the blood of all the Howards may flow in his veins,
shakes their hands so condescendingly at the time
of election, but, when that is over, ignores their
very existence so far as he is able. But, not to
digress from Sir Percy to such a very common
subject as Radical principles and contested elections. Although Sir Percy was a man whom the

Radicals of our times would emphatically, if not elegantly, designate "a bloated aristocrat;" as I have just said, the hauteur and reserve of his bearing and manner arose from the very fact that he knew so well that he was Sir Percy Percy, and understood so fully the duties which were imposed upon him by his position. Of course, I don't mean to affirm that he may not have over-valued his position, just as he may have over-estimated the duties which he conceived to devolve upon him by reason of that position; but, I am quite sure that he always acted as he *felt* himself bound to act, and, although, he was often very obstinate and very wrong-headed, I am equally certain that he never *thought* himself to be either the one or the other. He was one of those men who, in the most important actions of life, will act in a manner which is perfectly incomprehensible to others, although they themselves cannot conceive that it was possible for them to have acted otherwise than they did. Full of honour, and yet full of obstinacy; full of prejudice, prejudice the most unreasonable, and yet, at the same time, gentlemen in every sense of the word; with an overweening idea of their own rights and of their own dignity, and doing the wrongest things with the best intentions; such men exist to be enigmas to themselves, and, most probably, sources of misery to all with whom they are brought into contact in the closer relations of domestic life or service.

Such a man was Sir Percy Percy, in the fullest sense of the word, and, as in the course of this story I shall have to narrate some very painful circumstances, in which it will be hard to acquit him of blame, and as I shall not hesitate, in its due place, to speak of him strongly and harshly, I am all the more glad to have an opportunity of here expressing the conviction which I always entertained, that he was honourable and true; that I always believed that he was acting in the manner which *he* considered right, and as the only course open to him, even in circumstances in which I am certain in my very heart that he was as wrong, and as unjust, and as harsh as it is possible for a man to be; circumstances so utterly painful and sad, so full of the bitterest and most poignant memories for me, that, although I may forgive him his part in them, I can never forget either him or that part; never think of him with those kindly feelings with which I would wish to regard every one who has passed away for ever from the earth, and gone to render to the eternal Judge of all, his account of those actions which cast a deadly blight upon lives ten thousand times more pure, more promising, more priceless than his own.

When I have added that he was as uncompromising in religion as in politics, a man who, whilst he either forgot or ignored the fact, that those very ancestors of whom he was most proud, and whose names shone most conspicuously in the annals of their country, had often fought, and sometimes died, in the defence of the Catholic faith of olden times, considered the Protestant religion as the peculiar glory of his native land, a religion for which every gentleman, and, most of all, every conservative gentleman, was bound to spill the last drop of his blood, I think I have said all that is necessary, in this place, of my host, Sir Percy Percy.

At the time of my visit the eldest son, the heir to the estates, was absent on his travels. The present Lady Percy was not the mother of Eustace and his elder brother. Their mother had died some few months after the birth of Eustace, and, after remaining a widower for many years, Sir Percy had married again, about two years previous to the period of which I am writing. This marriage had given great offence to Rupert, the eldest son, more especially as Lady Percy had already borne her husband a child, a boy, who, at the time of my visit to the Hall, was some months old. It was said that very hot words had been interchanged on the subject of this marriage between Sir Percy and his eldest son, who by no means relished the prospect of his father making provision for a young family out of the estates, and that, after the interview, the young man had left home, declaring that he would never return until he returned to take possession in his own right.

I had never seen Lady Percy, but, of course, I was introduced to her that evening in the drawing-room before dinner. When I entered the apartment she was standing by the fireplace in conversation with her husband. Sir Percy came to meet me, and, taking me by the arm, led me across the room, and introduced me to his wife. I am sure that I was very awkward, and that I blushed very much, as boys fresh from school are apt to do; but I paid my respects as gracefully and with as much ease as I was able, and, that over, I raised my eyes to look at my hostess. She seemed to me to be some twenty years younger than her husband. She was magnificently dressed, and I thought at the moment that she was the handsomest lady whom I had ever seen; and yet, from that very first moment I could *not* like her. It was a case of one of those unaccountable and unreasonable repugnances which we feel every now and then, and which, the more we investigate them, seem all the more unreasonable, but which, after we have fully convinced ourselves, by acute argument, of their utter absurdity, we find, to our intense astonishment, more deeply seated in our souls than ever. As she turned her large, black eyes upon me, there seemed to me to be a cold glitter in them which chilled me to the heart. Her smile was very bright and pleasant, and her voice was very soft and gentle, whilst the language which she employed was always ladylike in the highest degree. When she spoke to me and Eustace of our schoolboy days, of our amusements, and on other subjects which would naturally please us, she did so in words which, in themselves, should express interest and sympathy; and yet, I could never get over the idea that she was only *pretending*. Sometimes I was quite angry with myself for my unreasonable conduct, but it was no use, I couldn't help it. And even if I did ever succeed in arguing myself into a more becoming state of mind, one glance of her cold eyes was enough to put all my good resolutions to flight, and make me as unreasonable as before. It was plain to me at once that Sir Percy was very fond of her, and that she exercised great influence over him. She seemed, too, to be equally attached to him; but here, again, I was as foolish as ever, for I could not persuade myself of her sincerity even in this. If I wronged her I am very sorry for it, for, to all outward show, she was as beautiful a lady as her husband was a noble-looking and gallant gentleman; but, spite of my best endeavours, I could never altogether conquer the involuntary shrinking from her which I experienced from the first time I met her, or persuade myself that she was not, for some purpose of her own, acting a part— a part which she sustained with admirable skill and naturalness, through all the varied duties and occupations of her life.

My Lady was a model stepmother to Eustace,

and, yet, I never shrank so much from her, or felt such an involuntary dislike to, and distrust of her, as I did at those times when she called my friend to her, and made him sit at her feet, whilst she put away his hair from his brow, and kissed him as tenderly *to all appearance* as his own dead mother might have done. It was a strange feeling, and one for which I was heartily ashamed of myself at the time; but I never saw her fondling him that I did not think of a sleek panther, or some other animal of an equally treacherous nature, playing with its prey; and I could not help entertaining a most earnest and ardent desire that my friend might never fall into her power, that she might never have an opportunity of injuring him, or of doing him an evil turn.

Of course I kept these strange feelings or prejudices of mine buried a profound secret in my own breast. I was so much afraid of them that I think I never voluntarily entertained them—they forced themselves upon me against my will. Hence, I should never have dared to put them into words, or have expressed them to any living being, and, least of all, to my dear friend, if he had not himself first led me to speak of them. Towards the end of my visit, one evening, after we had retired for the night, Eustace came to my room, and sat down by my fire. For a little while we talked on indifferent subjects, but, by degrees, our conversation turned to my visit, and to Sir Percy and his lady. As a matter of course, I spoke in the highest terms of Percy Grange, of the pleasant days which I had spent in it, and of its host and hostess. Eustace was sitting directly opposite to me, and, as I rattled on with hot, enthusiastic words about the dignity of Sir Percy, and the beauty and kindness of his wife, I could not help remarking that there was a strangely sad and perplexed look upon the face of my friend. At last he came over to me, and put his hand upon my shoulder, and looked down into my face as he had often done before in his moments of doubt and of perplexity, or when we were more than usually earnest and confidential with one another.

"Ambrose," he said, suddenly, and jerking out his words in a manner that was very unusual with him, " Ambrose, I'm going to ask you a strange question, and a question which I would not have put to another being on earth but yourself. What do you think of my Lady?"

My heart gave one great beat in my breast as the words which he spoke with such strange earnestness—an earnestness which seemed to me not unmingled with fear and dread, fell upon my ear. Without a moment's hesitation, only waiting till I had taken his other hand in both of mine, I returned his earnest, searching glance, and answered him in words which rose instinctively to my lips:—

"Eustace, I don't like my Lady. I don't know why, but I'm afraid of her. Spite of her soft words and her beautiful face, she chills me to the very heart. I'm sure it's very unreasonable, and I'm almost ashamed of myself for harbouring such a prejudice, still I can say nothing but the truth to *you*, Eustace. Perhaps it would have been better if you had not asked me this question, but the truth is, my dear fellow, that I *don't* like my Lady, and that I fear as much as I dislike her."

It seemed so preposterous, even to myself, that I should presume to speak in this manner, although it was only to Eustace, of one so rich, so handsome, and so much admired as my Lady Percy, that I instinctively glanced at the door as I uttered these words in a low, trembling voice. I think I almost expected to see her sweep in, in all the majestic beauty of her stately presence, her large, black eyes, usually so cold, flashing fire, and her whole form swelling with pride and indignation. I need scarcely add that my Lady did not make her appearance, and when I had recovered from the fright into which I had been thrown by my own boldness and audacity, I cannot tell how much I felt relieved, or how heavy a weight seemed to have been moved from my heart, now that I had unburthened myself of that which had pressed so painfully upon me, now that I was aware that Eustace felt as I did, and that, consequently, he would be upon his guard if my Lady should ever try to play him false.

Eustace sighed heavily once or twice, and I felt the hand that rested on my shoulder tremble, as he pressed it more firmly to me, as if he signified by this motion that he leant more than ever upon my stronger will, that he relied more than ever upon my aid and support—an aid and support which, God knows, I would have laid down my life most cheerfully to give him; and then he took a chair, and sat down by my side.

"I'm very thankful to you, Ambrose," he said, at last, after sitting in silence for some time, " I'm very thankful to you for speaking to me so openly and so candidly, but it was only what I might have expected from your long and tried friendship." I pressed his hand, and he went on. " I can't tell you how I have striven and fought against these feelings of dislike and distrust with which I cannot help regarding my Lady. When I first experienced them I was horrified by their presence in my soul. It seemed to me so wrong to have anything but love and duty in my heart towards my father's wife, that I strove my best, my very best, to overcome them, and yet, spite of all my efforts, I could not drive these troublesome thoughts away. I could not make myself love her. I could not bring myself to regard her as holding towards me, in any degree or shape, the place of my own dead mother. She always speaks kindly to me, and yet I shrink from her. She is profuse in her gifts to me, and yet I feel an instinctive impulse to throw them away. She kisses me, and calls me her child, and, God forgive me," he cried, burying his face in his hands, and trembling with the emotion under which he laboured, " God forgive me for it, if I sin, I seem to loathe her from my inmost heart. Her kisses fill me with disgust; they seem to sicken my very soul; and yet, what can I do, what can I do?" he cried, in pitiable agitation. " I have no tangible grounds for this strange repugnance. I cannot point to a word or action of hers which would, of itself, justify me in entertaining feelings of dislike to her, and so I am constrained to continue to act in a manner which makes me despise myself. I pretend to feel what in my heart I do not feel. I show her the respect which she has a right as my father's wife to expect at my hands, but I also treat her with a semblance of affection which I do not feel, but the absence of which I dare not avow, utterly unreasonable, utterly unbecoming as it seems to be. I have never had but one secret from you, Ambrose," he continued, " and it has been this. I durst not tell this even to you, but it has grown so heavy of late, my burthen has become so unbearable, I am so miserable and so wretched at the presence of these unholy feelings in my soul, that I could bear it no longer, and so I have unbosomed myself to you, that you may help me by your advice and counsel to overcome myself, that you may tell me what I ought to do. God only knows how wretched this has made me."

He struggled bravely with himself to get the mastery over the emotions which were stirring so strongly in his breast, but, spite of all his efforts, every now and then a great sob rose in his throat; every now and then a wild appeal to God burst from his lips, to guide and direct him how to act, to keep him in the never-failing paths of duty and of truth. As for me, I could only do my best to comfort him with such words as my love and tender, deep compassion for him suggested to me. I would fain have told him that his misgivings, his distrust, his repugnance, were all unreasonable and without foundation, but I could not say that. Although my own ideas on this most painful matter had as little, nay, perhaps, even less real, tangible foundation than his own, still, I felt as he felt, and I could not say, not even for the purpose of consoling *him*, that which I did not believe to be the truth. Moreover, I felt an earnest craving in my heart to guard him from all possible harm; and, as it appeared to me to follow as a kind of necessary consequence to this, that he should be ever on the watch against my Lady, how could I counsel him to banish that distrust, to drive away those misgivings, which, by keeping him constantly on the alert, would be his surest protection, if she should ever attempt to injure him? Hence, if I had acted like a man simply under the guidance of reason, seeing that neither he nor I had any tangible grounds, any proofs which would bear examining by the light of that reason, for these misgivings and these fears of ours, I should have counselled him to cast them to the winds of heaven. But I did not act like a man simply guided by reason. Where *he* was concerned, my heart had always more sway over me than my cold reason; and, whilst my reason and my principles stepped in to define the limits of my affection and friendship for him, and to keep it within honest, manly, holy bounds, it was my heart which prompted me and taught me how to love him, taught me how to appreciate his noble qualities, bound me to him with a chain whose every link was one of truthful, honest friendship. Therefore, in this matter I acted towards him as my heart and not my reason prompted me; and whilst I did my best to comfort him in his trouble, I did not seek to remove his misgiving or mistrust. I only strove to show him that, at present, he laboured under a mere dread of evils which might never be realized, a repugnance which might turn out to be utterly unreasonable and without foundation, and which, therefore, ought not to give him any present trouble, provided he prayed to God to remove them, if it were His holy will, provided he did not give them any undue encouragement, or listen needlessly to them. If I had given my friend any other counsel than this, as, in that moment of solemn confidence he held my hands so lovingly and so confidingly in his own, I should have acted against all the promptings of my heart and love; and, although the assertion may, perhaps, be false, and whilst I am quite sure there are many who will repudiate it, and reject it as altogether untenable and unworthy of rational men, I am by no means certain that, in a matter such as this, and between friends bound together as we were, the heart, provided it be truthful and honest, is not quite as safe and trustworthy a counsellor as the head.

In a little while he grew calmer, and spoke to me more in detail about his feelings, and his fears of his stepmother. "We have never had any quarrel," he went on to say. "Nay, she always treats me with apparent affection; but yet, although I can scarcely describe it, there is a change in our family, a change which is very evident to me, and one which helps to fill me with an indefinable dread of impending evil, since she entered it. Rupert has gone abroad, after parting from my father in fierce and bitter anger; and Sir Percy makes no secret that he will cause my brother to feel the full weight of his indignation; and, although the family estates are strictly entailed, still there are many ways in which he can interfere with the property, if he be so disposed. Whenever my father speaks against Rupert, my

Lady pretends to take his part; but you know, Ambrose," he continued, "she only pretends to do it. I am sure she only pretends; and, in the end, my father is always more angry and more incensed than before. My father and I have never had any disagreement, and yet he is not the same to me that he was before she came here. He is more exacting, more distant in his manner; and all the affection that is left in him seems to be lavished on her. At all events," he went on, his low, sad voice growing sadder every moment, "he bestows none of it on me. I love him with all my heart and soul, and I am as proud of him as any one can be of such a noble and true gentleman as he is, but I miss sadly the loving words and the loving care which he used to bestow on us before she came. You know, Ambrose," he went on, "although he was very distant and reserved to the world outside, he was never so to Rupert and me in former days. No boys could have had a dearer or more affectionate father than we had, but it is all changed now. Rupert is an exile, and, for me, I don't know when my turn may come. For some time past I have felt as if the shadow of a great trouble were upon me, and the more I try to shake it off the more it presses upon me, and the darker it becomes. I don't complain, God knows I don't complain because he loves the wife whom he has brought home to us. Still less do I complain because he loves his little child, for he does not love him more dearly than I do; but I think his heart might hold us all. Oh! surely, his heart might hold us all."

His voice died away in a sob, as once more he turned to me for comfort, and consolation, and support. I did my best to comfort him, as one brother may comfort another, in those solemn occasions which arise, perhaps, once or twice in a life, and in which the tongue has no words to express what the heart would fain speak. After a while, however, I said a few words to him, not many, for my heart was too full for much speech; but still, sufficient to tell him yet again that he was dear to me above all price; almost as dear as she to whom I owed my being, she who claimed my best and purest love—to tell him that, in weal or woe, in sickness or in health, in pleasure or in pain, I would ever be as faithful and as true a friend to him as God, who saw my heart, knew that I was in that moment of sacred communing, in that moment of confidence so solemn and so sad, in that moment of doubt and of dread so undefined, and yet so bitter and so deep.

As I looked into his fair, young face, and into the full, blue eyes, which spoke of nothing but of purity and truth; as I looked upon the golden glory of his long, bright hair, whilst I soothed him almost as I would have done if he had been a little child; how could I think that, as he had whispered to me, the shadow of a great trouble was upon him? How could I believe that trouble, or care, or pain, were ever meant to fall athwart *his* path? But, although I saw it not, the shadow was there, full, dark, menacing, and close at hand. The clouds were lowering round about him, ready to burst in all the fury of the coming storm upon his head, whilst I, who would have taken any trouble to shield him from a moment's harm, was as powerless to discern its approach as I was impotent to help him when, in all its force, it broke upon him, and seethed and raged in angry waves about his darkened path—a path upon which God alone could shed one ray of light, or make one whit less rugged or less thorny to his bleeding feet.

CHAPTER IV.

ILLUSIONS AND DIGRESSIONS.

My first and last visit to Percy Grange soon came to a close; and, notwithstanding the condescension of Sir Percy, the kindness of my Lady, and my own natural inclination and desire to be in the company of my friend Eustace, I was very glad to return to my own more humble home, where I spent the remainder of my vacation with my mother. I ought to mention that, before I left the Hall, Sir Percy, without actually pledging himself, gave me to understand that, in the event of my taking orders, he would present me to the rectory of Percymoate on the next vacancy; and, as the clergyman who now held the living was far advanced in years, this promise of his (if I could so call it) opened to me a prospect much more satisfactory, and even brilliant, than I could ever have aspired to, if left to my own unaided efforts to advance myself in life. Whilst my heart was full of gratitude to him for his kindly interest in my welfare, and this almost more for my mother's sake than my own, I concluded, perhaps not altogether without foundation, that I had established myself pretty firmly in his good graces, and that I was a decided favourite of his. The words with which he notified his intention to me were, indeed, almost as cold and frigid as those which he habitually employed; but, I knew him well enough by this time not to judge him altogether by his manner or his mere words; and when, in the excess of my gratitude, I so far forgot his stately presence as to seize his hand, and kiss it impetuously, whilst I stammered out some blundering words of thankfulness and of never-dying recollection of his goodness towards me, there was a tremor in his voice as he told me that he would willingly do more than this for my father's son, which made me think that there were chords, even in his heart, which vibrated to the memories of the past—chords which, perchance, were but seldom touched, but which, when touched, responded all the more deeply, all the more truly, at the call of Nature, the great master-hand, by very reason that the notes which they contained, whether of pleasure or of pain, were thus seldom evoked, or allowed to make themselves heard beyond the secret and hidden recesses of the sensitive, or the proud and haughty heart. I could not help thinking, too, that cold, haughty, and passionless, as he seemed to be, there had been a time when he and my dead father were friends, no less faithful and true than were now his own son and the son of his early friend. At all events, I parted from him, on my return to my mother's cottage, with all my former veneration and respect for him increased a thousand fold by the appreciation of his goodness towards me, which was now added to those sentiments. I should have thought him perfection if I could have forgotten those sad words of my friend, which were still ringing in my ears: "His heart might hold us all; oh, surely, his heart might hold us all;" and, although the recollection of the change which he had allowed to come over him since his marriage, in regard to his elder children, lowered him somewhat in my estimation, still, as I blamed my Lady a good deal more than him for even this, I parted from him with a feeling of respectful veneration for himself, and with such a deep and sincere appreciation of what I deemed his high and noble qualities, as would have endured to the end of my life if, at a later period, by his own heartless and cruel indifference to one whom he ought to have cherished with his heart's best love,—if, by his own harsh and unreasonable severity, he had not destroyed the delusion and scattered it to the winds. There are, I think, few things more painful, even in a world which is full of pain, than the destroying of those illusions which the heart, either in its simplicity or its love, has built up with such a profuse expenditure of its best affections on the object loved; with such a keen and jealous appreciation of those qualities, either real or fancied, which it believes its idol to

possess; with such a lavish forgetfulness of self and
selfish interest in its yearning anxiety to pour itself
out, with all that it has, on him whom it deems
so worthy of its truest love, its fairest hope, its
deepest and its never-dying care. And then, when
the appointed time, which, sooner or later, is almost certain to come, has arrived, and the love
which seemed so changeless has been blown away
by the first rude breath which fell upon it; when
the summer heat has withered up, or the autumn
blast has blighted, ruthlessly and unsparingly, the
flowers which looked so pleasant and so fair whilst
the dew of early spring was resting on their leaves,
and nestling in their half-blown buds; when the
experience and the wisdom of growing years sit
down in judgment to condemn with such wise
saws, such heartless sneers, such cold and cutting
words, the ill-judged sympathies and affections of
those earlier and, in truth, those better and those
purer days,—ah, me! it is a weary and a bitter task,
and one at which strong men may well falter and
grow pale, to demolish at one fell blow the baseless
fabric which till then had seemed so strong and
firm, to sweep away and utterly wipe out the delusion which till then had seemed so true and deep,
and which, when it has gone, will surely leave a
void which all the coming years will never fill
again. Yes, this demolishing and sweeping away
of our illusions is, in truth, a weary and a com-
fortless task, but one which, I fear me much, we

are most of us called upon to perform oftener than is at all pleasant; a task which is none the less hateful, none the less to be trembled and shuddered at, because it is as unavoidable as it is full of painful and of sorrowful regrets. I was called upon in later days to demolish thus ruthlessly the very innocent delusion which, in my inexperience, I had fallen into regarding Sir Percy Percy. I discovered later on that he was not all that I had fancied him, all that I had imagined him to be; and would that this had been the most bitter discovery which, in the battle of life, I was ever called upon to make; oh, would that this had been the strongest and most dearly-cherished illusion which I was ever called upon to annihilate and sweep away. But, no more of this. I will only add with the poet, that—

> "The apprehension of the good
> Gives but the greater feeling to the worse :
> Fell sorrow's tooth doth never rankle more
> Than when it bites, but lanceth not the sore."

At the close of our vacation my friend and I entered Oxford. I, of course, was bound to a certain fixed college, and consequently had no choice in this matter. Sir Percy willingly allowed his son to enter the same college as myself, although he might have reasonably preferred that his son should be in a more aristocratic house than that in which my Exhibition entitled me to take up my abode. Tom Bowman came down on the same day as ourselves, and a very hearty, and a very pleasant meeting we had. However, I saw at a glance that the friendship of Atherby school was somewhat in danger. I knew well enough that there would be no change between Eustace and me, but Tom had put his name on the books of the " fastest" college in Oxford; and as I was very much afraid that Tom was likely to be the fastest amongst the fast, I thought that he would be pretty sure to travel at a much more lively pace than either my means or my inclinations would allow me to take. I knew well enough that his " set" would never suit me on pecuniary grounds, even if on no other, and I was sure that it would suit Eustace less. I was equally sure that I would do my best to keep Eustace out of it; for, although he was incomparably purer and better than I, still, ridiculous as it may seem, I always considered myself, in a certain sense, as his guardian; and, whilst probably I should merely have laughed off any attempt to lead myself astray, I should have repelled the same attempt, if it had been made upon him, with the angry word, and, as likely as not, the hasty blow. Hence, as I saw that Tom would necessarily have to choose between his old friends and his new ones, and although I had little doubt that, whilst his better feelings would be in favour of the old ones, he would be carried captive by the new ones, as well through his own inclinations, as by the greater attractions which he would find in their company, and by their more showy qualities, I was quite prepared to find a considerable falling off in our former intimacy, or, at all events, in the outward manifestation of it, and in this I was not disappointed. I have, however, written those words " the outward manifestation of it" advisedly, for I believe that there was never any change in his heart. I believe that in his heart he was ever the same, and that, although he might sometimes leave us for days without dropping into our rooms, the hours which he *did* spend with us in our own quiet way were the happiest, as they were the most dearly cherished by him. I believe that, although he had not strength of will to break away from the new companions who got such hold upon him, he always wished to do it; and I am sure that, in his better moments, his heart always instinctively turned away with disgust from the noisy band who surrounded him, and played, I do not say maliciously, but, at all events, thoughtlessly and heedlessly, upon his pliant nature, to the friends of his earlier days. However, as I shall have to speak of him again shortly, I will say no more on this point, except that, as at Atherby school, Tom had always been the leader in everything that was daring or out of order, so, at Oxford, whether an unpopular dean were to be screwed up in his room, an obnoxious proctor to be persecuted within an inch of his life, or a battle-royal to be organized between Town and Gown, Tom Bowman was certain to be the heart and soul of the undertaking.

As I must hasten on to other and more important matters, I have no intention of giving my reader any detailed account either of the grand old city itself, or of our life during the time we were privileged to spend within the walls, whose every stone seems to speak with a deathless voice of the glories of those ancient days, when England's faith brought forth such goodly fruit, and raised aloft such noble homes, where sanctity and science might settle and take root, as may, perchance, still plead her cause before God, as may, perchance, be allowed to stand in some small measure against the errors and prevarications of the evil times on which her lot has fallen. It seems to me as if the very stones of such a place as Oxford must for ever cry aloud to us to remember the days of old and the generations which have passed away— to remember the days when England's kings and England's princes deemed their faith the brightest jewel in their crown—the days when there was, through all the land, but the one altar as there was but the one true faith—the days when Mary's name was a "household word," and "Mary's dower" was one of England's proudest titles—the days when Englishmen could bend in willing and in happy submission to the dictates of their conscience and their faith—a faith that was obedient, and rational because it was obedient—the days of faith that were happy and were blessed *because* they were days of faith,—a faith which spoke in works, which raised for the worship of God Westminster, and Hereford, and York, and the rest of the glorious churches which cast such a solemn and a moving beauty on our waving fields and on our smiling valleys; a beauty which is all the more touching now, because it is so mournful, too; the beauty of the fair body which has not as yet seen corruption on its outward form, but which, nevertheless, has lost the living soul, which gave it half its beauty and all its life—a faith which raised and which endowed such stately homes, where holy men might teach, and studious youth might learn, as Oxford and as Cambridge —a faith which ever set aside its richest fields and its most fertile lands for the monastery and the abbey, which, even in their ruins, are ten thousand times more grand and fair than the stately workhouses which have taken their place, and in which the Gothic windows and the fanciful spires that grace the exterior, are supposed to be compensation enough to God's blessed poor for the harsh rule which reigns inside,—compensation enough to console the aged pair who have been so foully parted, although the minister of God told them when they stood before the altar, in the trusting confidence of their life's young spring, that God had joined them together, and that no man should put them asunder; that aged pair who, after a long life of labour and of duty, truly and faithfully done in their own humble sphere, would fain go down the hill together side by side, would fain tend one another, even to the last. Ah! God help ye, my poor brethren, when such a pitiful boon as this may not be granted to you;—God help ye, in the evil days on which you have fallen, when short-sighted men forget that you are far dearer than themselves, with all their riches and their gewgaws, in the sight of God; when they would fain put you out of the way altogether if they could, but, being obliged to tolerate you, stow you away in houses that are fair to look upon outside, that you may be as little offensive to their daintiness as is compatible with the fact of your existence; that your prison house may, exteriorly, at least, remind them as little as possible of poverty and of suffering, and of all such unpleasant things; and, this end secured, why should they trouble themselves because the children, whose curse it is to come into the world beneath such roofs, are tainted—tainted did I say? —nay, steeped in the foul leprosy which is born of places such as these, almost as soon as they can speak—children, upon whose cheeks the fair hues of childhood are never seen,—children whose tongues have never uttered a gentle or a loving speech, but whose first words have been the curse which sounds so fearfully upon the childish lips, and whose first responsible acts have been acts of sin and shame? Why should they trouble themselves because these children of corruption grow up to add each one its own foul share to the mass which festers all around us, and which grows each day more unmanageable, more beyond the control of magistrates and of law-makers; threatening to bring down upon us a ruin which we are impotent to stave off, but which, in its approach, is causing honest, earnest men no little fear, no little dread and apprehension? Why should they trouble themselves because this mighty land of ours, with all her wealth and all her boundless resources, with all that pure religion of which she talks so much, and which she labours so unceasingly to spread abroad, can devise no happier home for her worn-out poor than a parish workhouse; where the faithful hearts which fought the battle of the world so long together may be rent asunder at the very last; may be left to pine away in that saddest solitude of all, the solitude of the heart; may be brought to such sorrow and such bitter care that they never seek or never leave their miserable beds without begging God to take them out of the evil place, to take them to Himself at once? Ah, God help ye, my poor brethren, and God help us all, when we have nothing but workhouses with Gothic gables and pitched roofs; nothing but the harsh word and the harsher treatment of those who only serve you with an unwilling hand, and because they are paid to do it; nothing but the pauper's miserable funeral and the pauper's miserable grave to give you, in place of the watchful care which, in the blessed days gone by, sought you at the convent's gate; which led you in and tended you with such a loving hand, because you were one of God's own blessed poor, and because the sister who waited by your side saw her Master's image reflected forth in you; which closed your eyes with such a reverent touch; which laid you in your hallowed grave with holy mass and solemn rite; which placed the cross above the spot where you slept in faith, and peace, and rest; which loved you none the less in life; which prized your memory none the less in death, because you were one of those whom He who cannot lie, He before whose eternal justice all things shall be set right in the time to come, has declared to be "blessed" with an everlasting blessing amongst the sons of men.

CHAPTER V.

THE "NATURAL MAN."

I HAVE said that I did not intend to trouble my reader with any long history of Oxford or Oxford life, and I intend to keep that promise, more especially as in the last chapter I relapsed into an old transgression of mine, and rambled away from the chain of my story into several digressions, which digressions may, perhaps, form links, more or less elegant, or quite the contrary, in the embellishing of that chain, but which are in no wise necessary for its due construction. Besides, I dare say that Oxford life is considerably changed from what it was in my days; and there are plenty of works to be had which will give the reader a much clearer insight than I could pretend to do into the present state of things at that great seat of learning. For example, he who is anxious to view Oxford from an æsthetical and controversial point of view may surely satisfy himself to the full in " Loss and Gain," a work from the master-hand of one who, more deeply, perhaps, than any other in these later times, entered into the heart and soul of that great storehouse of learning; who appreciated more

keenly, perhaps, than any other all that Oxford
had been in the olden times, all that she might be,
and all that she ought to be; and who, as he loved
her with all the freshness, the truth, and the depth
of his younger days, with a love which every noble
and right-hearted man must feel for his early
school, and still more, perchance, for his college
or university, still loves her with an affection, it
may be, somewhat more chastened and sad, but
not one whit the less fresh, the less true, or the
less deep, in the growing years of his honoured
life—a life, each year of which adds one measure
more to that mild dignity, and that imperishable
renown which for evermore shall be linked with
his name in every Catholic, and in many a Protestant heart.

Yes, by all means, let him who desires to see
Oxford under what I may, somewhat distorting
the word, call a spiritual point of view, read " Loss
and Gain," whilst he whose curiosity is turned in
the direction of " muscular Christianity," as exhibited and developed under certain phases of
Oxford life, may also satisfy his cravings by reading the history of one " Tom Brown," who,
although he turned out a great deal more snobbish
and less interesting as an Oxford undergraduate
than he promised to do when he first came under
our notice as a frank, generous, dashing, thoroughly
English schoolboy, will, nevertheless, afford the
reader a very fair idea of what I understand to be

the career and manner of life of the greater number of those who now-a-days enter the walls of the university.

But, although for these and other reasons I shall not enter minutely into my own Oxford life, as such, or that of my friends, I must, nevertheless, delay you for some little time on this matter, as it was during our stay in the university that an event occurred which, although it may not be very interesting to the reader, was of overwhelming importance to Eustace and myself; which gave a colour to all our coming life; which threw upon our, or, at all events, upon his path shadows which, at one time, threatened never to clear away, and which, before the day of brightness came at last, after long and weary looking for, enveloped him in such a storm of trouble and of pain, dragged him through such years of weary anxiousness and blighting care, rained down such trials and such fierce afflictions on his head as, I pray God, may never fall to mortal man again, and, least of all, to one so gentle and so mild, so sensitive and so shrinking from the world's cold blasts, so little able to battle with the ills and woes of this changing life, as was poor Eustace Percy. From all that I have said of him, and from my feeble endeavours to give a sketch of his character, at once so deep and so enthusiastic, so pure and so true, my reader will have no difficulty in believing me when I assert that Eustace was a youth of deep religious convictions, and of a moral, irreproachable life. I don't mean to say that he was holy or perfect in our Catholic sense of those words,—how could he have been so? We had spent our early days in Atherby school amid all the levity and, to use the mildest word for it, the unreflecting thoughtlessness of word and act which is born, and necessarily born, of institutions such as these, where a large number of boys, or rather young men, are thrown together without any fixed principles to guide them; without any one to whom they can lay open their hearts, or from whom they may seek counsel in times of doubt and of temptations from within or without; where the only rule of life which is brought before them comes in the shape of the unmeaning generalities which form, I think I may say without uncharitableness or desire to wound any one, the staple of the sermons which are delivered from the pulpits of the Church by law established, or, certainly, by those members of it who belong either to the High and Dry, or Low and Broad schools; and these were the schools which were, I think, the most common in our younger days, although they might not be known by these names. At all events, I am pretty certain that the sermons which were delivered from the pulpit of Atherby Church were not adapted, from their nature, to have much influence over, or effect upon such auditors as the boys of Atherby school. The poor curate, to whom we were doomed to listen for, at least, nine months in the year, was about one of the most uninteresting pulpit orators under whom a congregation was ever condemned, in punishment for its sins, to sit. I think he had a certain number of sermons either in print or manuscript, and that he used to go over these regularly and methodically, beginning at the beginning, and working his way gradually through them till he came to the end of his stock, when he commenced afresh at the beginning, and this, year after year, until we were sick to death of them. He used to preach the same sermon several times every year; and it was said that the old parish clerk had heard them delivered so often, and in such regular order, that he could always tell what sermon would be delivered on any particular Sunday. Now, these sermons, as far as I recollect them, were dry disquisitions on the most general topics, and although they may have been all very well in themselves, and, in a literary point of view, may have done credit as "Essays" on religious subjects to the composer of them, whoever he may have been; still, merely read to us as they were, and that in the most dry and unimpassioned manner, it was not in the nature of things that they should have had any effect upon a number of youths just springing into early manhood, in teaching them how, and, most of all, in persuading them to endeavour to combat and repress their passions, in inculcating upon them in a

H

forcible manner those great truths which can alone be safe foundations upon which to build, in reducing and applying those generalities to practical and individual cases; and the curate of Atherby never went beyond " generalities." This was all the positive instruction, if it may be called by such a name, which we received. We were, indeed, obliged to read the Bible for a certain time every Sunday evening, but I am quite sure that the spiritual profit derived from this exercise was but small; and how could it have been otherwise, unable as we were to understand the difficult passages in the sacred writings, and so little prepared to enter upon their perusal with those dispositions which are absolutely required in the reader, that he may derive spiritual advantage and profit from such perusal. On Sunday evenings the head master of the school frequently delivered an address, or exhortation, or whatever you may wish to call it, to us; but he generally kept clear of purely religious matters, and confined himself to the inculcating of honour amongst ourselves, truth towards our superiors and one another, and those general principles which are supposed to form a frank, honest, open, truthful boy. But, although these are all noble qualities, much to be commended, and much to be employed in the training of youth, yet, if they are inculcated as merely natural virtues, as was the case with the master of our school in his addresses to us, they will hardly guide a boy into the way of perfection, or bring forth much fruit of positive sanctity in him. I am quite certain that Eustace was by far the most religious and the most perfect youth in the school, but I am equally certain that he was far from perfect, in the true and Catholic sense of the word; and, with the training which he had received, how could it have been otherwise? Where was he to have learnt that purity of intention; that reference of all his thoughts, words, and actions to God; that union of his heart with his Creator; that delicateness of conscience, which will shrink instinctively from even the approach of an unholy thought;—virtues which are all required in him who makes even his first step on the path of perfection; virtues which are known and practised, in a higher or lesser degree, by every Catholic youth who is faithful to his religion and his duty; but virtues whose very names, I fear me much, are scarcely known to many of those who wander on the broad and weary road of self-indulgence and of sin; those who are given up to the evil and the cursed guidance of their own fierce wills; those who are never taught, as God's blessed Catholic Church can alone teach them, to walk even in the hot blood of their early youth along the narrow paths of duty and of self-denial, the paths of prayer, of purity, and of Christian truth? Hence, although in the heart of Eustace Percy there certainly was, as, perhaps, there may also have been in the hearts of some few others, a yearning after something more holy and more perfect; a desire for those higher and those better things of which they had, God help them, but such vague and indistinct ideas, I am sure that the prevailing spirit of the school was one of levity, and I am afraid that I must add, one of sinfulness. And when I say this, I do not mean to reflect upon or to blame any one in particular. The system and the spirit of the place were radically wrong, and intrinsically false, untrue, and unenlightened by the grace of God, as the system and the spirit of all such places must necessarily be. Hence, I do not mean to reflect upon individuals, who, perhaps, acted towards us and did their duty according to their lights; but, what I mean to say and to maintain is that, until we reform, or, rather, do away with false systems of education, systems which do not regard religion, and, by religion I mean *true* religion, as the foundation of all education, we must not be astonished if such systems bring forth the fruit which is to be expected from them—fruits which corrupt and vitiate youth in what ought to be its freshest and its purest days—fruits which, in their ripening and their harvest, have broken many a mother's heart, and brought many a father's gray hairs with sorrow to the grave. And here I can fancy one of the readers who, although he may not think as I think, or believe as I believe, on many essential points, may, perhaps, have fallen upon this book, exclaiming, "Oh, I understand it all. This writer means to assert that youth can only be trained to, and kept in the ways of virtue and of purity through the agency of the Catholic Church, with the numberless influences which it can bring to bear upon the youthful mind and heart, and, most of all, through the agency of its confessional;" and, abstracting from particular cases into which I do not enter, and speaking merely to the general question, I at once candidly and most unreservedly assure such a reader that this is precisely what I *do* mean to assert.

I should not have entered into this matter at all, or in any shape whatever, although I deem it one of the last importance, if I had not thought it necessary for my purpose to do so. But, without these few remarks, I could scarcely have given my reader a fair idea of the state of mind in which Eustace and I entered Oxford. I believe that he passed through the fierce ordeal of Atherby school, as I have already said, as free from injury or taint as any boy who ever entered it. But I, who knew him well, knew him, indeed, better than any one else; I, who was deeper than any other in the confidences and secrets of his truthful, earnest, holy heart, knew well that he was thoroughly and profoundly dissatisfied. I knew that he was craving in his inmost soul after something to which he could give no name, but a something which was ever present to him,—a something which, as he

expressed it to me, would take him out of himself
and fix his heart upon the love and service of his
Maker. He was yearning with the instinctive
longing of a pure and simple heart after union
with his God, and there was no one to teach him
how that union was to be brought about; how the
obstacles were to be cleared away which, spite of
all his efforts, *would* come, as he often sadly said
to me, between him and God; no one to guide his
steps into the way of truth and life. I know with
what earnestness—with an earnestness, indeed, that
was painful to me to witness—he sought for light
and guidance in the vague generalities which fell
once a week from the lips of the poor, over-worked
curate of Atherby; and I know that he never
found what he sought, that he came away with
his heart empty, and his eyes enveloped in mists.
" I can make nothing out of it, Ambrose," he said
to me many and many time. " It's all mist and
confusion, but of this I am quite sure," he would
add with flashing eyes, and with a tongue trembling with emotion, "of this, I am quite sure, that
the Almighty never intended a man to live as,
God help me, I am living, and as I cannot live
much longer. I am quite sure," he would go on,
" that God intended me to believe something fixed
and defined, or else why should He threaten me
with damnation, as He does, if I do not believe all
things whatsoever He commanded his apostles to
teach. Now, what are those things which He

commanded His apostles to teach? That is what I cannot make out. That is what I cannot find any one to tell me, and yet, there must be some one, somewhere or other, who can teach me what I am to believe, who can teach me how I ought to live." When I, in my simplicity, suggested that, perhaps, Mr. Grant, the curate, might be this appointed teacher, poor Eustace would turn away with something that was as near akin to impatience as ever came from him. "I tell you, Ambrose, it's no use," he would retort in the same eager way which it so pained me to see in him; "I tell you, it's no use. I have listened to him with all my heart and soul, and I have prayed with all my heart and soul—God only knows how I have prayed—and yet it is all mist and darkness—God help me, it is all mist and darkness."

Poor, dear fellow, he little knew how near the light was to him—he little knew how lovingly and how mercifully God had listened to his simple prayers—he little knew the path that was opening before his feet—he little knew how powerfully and how efficaciously God's right hand was working to set all these crooked things straight when the fulness of the appointed time should have come!

Such was the state of mind in regard to religious matters with which Eustace took his leave of Atherby school. As for me, I was troubled with no such tormenting thoughts. Although I hope, I may venture to say for myself, that I had kept pretty clear of the worst phases of our school life, influenced as I had ever been most strongly by the example of my friend, and by the remembrance of some simple lessons which my mother, in her love, had taught me, still, I had never professed to be very good. I had never made any pretensions to piety. My heart had never been awakened to a desire for anything better, purer, or more holy than those things with which I was surrounded. I was quite content to take things as they were, without inquiring too closely into them. I was always ready enough to take my fill of pleasure, to gratify my inclinations to any reasonable extent, without either scruple of conscience or misgiving that I was doing wrong. I think I should have shrunk from excess of any kind; but, I am afraid, quite as much because such excess was ungentlemanly as because it was sinful. In a word, whilst my friend was striving in all the anguish and the earnestness of his awakened heart after that indefinable something which, day by day, was drawing him ever more strongly, more efficaciously to itself, I was living the life of the natural man, and was quite satisfied with it. If any one had asked me whether I was as good as I wished to be, of course I should have answered in the negative; but, still, there was no real desire in my heart of being any better; no real desire of drawing nearer to my Maker, of uniting my heart to the heart of Him in whom it was destined to find its rest at last. I had strong notions of what was gentlemanly and becoming, of what was palpably right, or palpably wrong. I thought it very base to lie, to steal, or wilfully to injure any one, just as I thought it mean and dishonourable not to do my best to thrash any one who insulted me, or took undue liberties with me or my friends. I thought it wrong to neglect my prayers, or to behave in an unbecoming manner in church, and these latter notions I had learnt, I am quite sure, with many others of a like nature, from my mother. I practised these virtues, if they may be so called, with more or less fidelity, and in a manner more or less vague and general. They made up the sum of my spiritual life, if I may be allowed to apply the term to such a life as was mine, a life, nevertheless, which gave me no uneasiness, and which never struck me as wanting in any essential ingredient necessary to form a Christian gentleman, which I certainly aspired to be, and which I, as certainly, considered that I was.

Thus we entered Oxford—one of us ill at ease with his own heart, utterly and completely dissatisfied with his own interior state, longing earnestly and truly for higher, holier, and better things;—the other, well satisfied with himself, and his own belongings, so long as no one could reproach him with open impiety, could say that he was either a liar or a thief, could point to any word or act of his which did not become him as a scholar and a gentleman. Upon him and upon me God's grace came pouring down at a time when we did not look for it, and in a manner and in a measure which we had never expected; came down upon us in such abundant and overflowing profusion that it drew our two hearts, almost without our knowing it, to Him for whose love and service they were alone created; and which, whilst it taught us what a holy and a blessed thing it is to rest in God, and how pleasant and how secure are the ways of those who walk along the paths of His holy Church, taught us also to love one another more dearly and more truly than we had ever done before, because it taught us how to love one another in God and for God.

CHAPTER VI.

THE MOVING OF THE WATERS.

THE next few pages of this narrative must, I am afraid, be somewhat controversial and dogmatic; but, courteous reader, please don't "skip" them. I know well what a mistake it is to introduce heavy controversy into the pages of a work like this, because for one who will peruse it, ninety-nine out of every hundred readers will as surely "skip" it, while my publisher charges me quite as much for the printing of this heavy matter as he does for those portions which contain, what I may consider to be, the most exciting or romantic parts of my story. But, unwilling as I am to run the risk of boring you, the thread of the narrative which I have taken in hand imperatively requires that I enter, in this place, at some little length, into matters which are of their nature rather heavy for general readers. But, if I have not succeeded by this time in enlisting your interest in, and sympathy for my narrative, to such an extent as to stimulate you to make a bold plunge at the few pages which are now to come, the whole thing must be a sad failure; and I have little hope that you will read even another line of a story at which I have laboured with a great deal of earnestness and more good will, that I might make it interesting to you; that by its means and through its simple agency I might, insensibly to yourself, draw you to the love of God and the practice of Christian virtue; motives which, I trust, have guided and influenced me in taking up my pen to write this tale, as I am quite sure they form the motives and the purpose of the series of which this work is but one. If some writers propose to themselves no higher purpose or aim than to *amuse* their readers, such a purpose can never be the end of the series of which this work is a unit; but, at the same time, I believe that virtue may be inculcated, and that the heart may sometimes be drawn to God as powerfully and efficaciously through the instrumentality of an amusing but innocent story, as through those other means which are more commonly employed, and more directly adapted for these purposes. Moreover, I am pretty certain, too, that many a one who will never take up a book treating professedly of purely spiritual matters, one who, perhaps, will seldom assist at public sermons, may be brought under the influence of grace, may have his heart touched, and his mind enlightened and turned towards virtue and its practice, through the means of a story which, while it will avoid all appearance of preaching, will never lose sight of the high and holy motives which should influence every Catholic writer; and which will contrive so to " gild" the pill that the patient who would have turned away from it at once, with utter disgust and with positive refusal, if it had been offered to him in its native bitterness, shall have it swallowed not only without repugnance, but even with positive relish, with licking of lips and longing for more, almost before he is aware of its presence on his tongue. And now, having let you thus far into my secrets, my motives, and my intentions, the least I can expect from you in return, gentle reader, is, that, with or without a gulp, according to the greater or less sweetness of your natural disposition, without any wry faces or shrugging of shoulders, you will faithfully read the next few pages of this story, although you are aware of the matter to be treated in them. To reconcile you still more to the dose, I promise faithfully to give you as little of it as ever I can consistently with my purpose in writing my book, and to make it as attractive and palatable as ever I am able.

I have already mentioned that Eustace Percy, Tom Bowman, and myself entered Oxford together, and that this was in 182—. We soon settled down to the mode of life which was either pointed out to us by our tastes and inclinations, or forced upon us by our position and circumstances. Whilst Tom was engaged in bullying or dodging proctors, in worrying the very life out of inoffensive deans and conscientious tutors, in driving studious men who lived near him to the verge of distraction by the continual racket which went on in his rooms, in violating every law which could be transgressed with impunity, and a great many which could not be so broken, and in leading what was, I am afraid, a very wild and a very reckless life,—whilst I was engaged in studying with all my power that I might carry off the highest university honours to which I could aspire,— Eustace gave himself every day more and more keenly, more and more earnestly, to the study of those religious questions which had already taken such a hold upon his mind. We were together for at least some time every day, and our friendship, whilst it became more manly in its nature and expression, became also more deep and earnest than ever. It was not very often he spoke to me of his religious opinions and views, partly, perhaps, because he saw instinctively that the subject was one in which I took little or no interest, except in so far as it concerned *him*, and partly, no doubt, because I could give him no assistance in his researches after truth, no aid in forming and developing his views; still, little as we spoke on this matter, I could not help seeing that, in the course of a few months, his views began to assume a definiteness and shape which they had never before possessed, and which seemed to give him great pleasure and satisfaction. Gradually, too, he began to speak to me more frequently on these subjects than he had hitherto done, and as I was always but too happy to give him any pleasure in my power, I seemed to take any interest in them which was but too often, I am afraid, only put on.

"Ambrose," he several times said to me at this period, his eyes flashing, and his whole face lighting up with the intensity of the feeling under which he laboured, "Ambrose, I think I begin to see my way at last. The mists of the weary past are beginning to clear away. Not, you know, that I am at all certain about many things which are almost as mysterious as ever; but, still, I have got ideas which I never had before. During all the time we were at Atherby, and ever since I came here, I could not clearly make out what I was bound to believe, and what I was not bound to believe. In fact, sometimes I could scarcely tell whether I was bound to believe anything at all or not. There have been times when everything has been so vague and indistinct that I have been tempted, oh, so grievously tempted, to throw it over altogether, and to give myself up to a life of pleasure, a life of indifference to all religion and all forms of religious belief; and yet," he continued, half musingly, as if he were speaking to himself almost as much as to me, "and yet, although I hardly know what it was, there has always been a something in my heart which has risen in revolt against this temptation to deliver myself to sin and indifference; something which has always urged me to stumble onwards, although my path may have been so dark that I could scarcely grope my way. I don't know why it has been so, or how it has been, but there has always, even in my weakest moments, been that something making itself felt within me, causing me to shrink with as much horror from indifference as from grievous positive sin. I know it is very strange," he would go on, his voice gradually sinking to a whisper, whilst those earnest eyes of his glowed with a light that was almost as painful as it was wonderful to see in one so young, "I know it is very strange, but it has always been so; and, from my inmost heart, I thank my God for His goodness and His mercy to me. Yes, I thank my God that it has always been thus with me—that He has always filled my heart with a desire of knowing Him and loving Him more truly than I have ever been able to do—and I trust in Him to bring me right at last, I trust in Him to bring me right at last."

He would repeat these last words several times over, and in such tones of earnest pleading with God, of burning confidence, and yet of trembling doubt, as filled me with a kind of mysterious dread, which, whilst it frightened me, drew me to him more wonderfully and more powerfully than ever. At such moments it almost seemed to me as if he were communing visibly and really with God, or with His holy angels. It almost seemed as if he were surrounded with an atmosphere of mystic but of holy influences, which were tangible and true as the air we breathed—influences which were unknown to me, which I had never felt, and which, on this very account, alarmed me the more when I saw them manifested in him. It was not until I had left my seat and gone over to him, and laid my hand upon his shoulder—not until, with a slight trembling, he had come to himself, and raised his face to me, and looked into my eyes with all that confidence, that generous trust which, as I have already said, I never saw in any eyes but his—not until I had felt his hand on mine, and heard him asking me in words, ineffably gentle in their tone, whether " it were not very, very strange," that I could fully shake off those unaccountable sensations which had been creeping over me, that I could realize to the full that he was still flesh and blood the same as I was, that the hand I still held was the hand of my friend, whom, although I could never love more truly, I was now beginning to prize and to revere more deeply, more ardently, aye, even more reverently, than I had ever done before. Then I would answer, "Yes, Eustace, my dear friend, it is very strange, God knows it is very strange, and I cannot tell what it means." But, whilst it was true that I could not tell what

it meant, it was in nowise strange if I had only
had light to see it. If I had only known how to
read the workings of that earnest, simple, childlike mind; if I had only known how to measure
the beatings of the heart that was as pure and
innocent as it was true and deep, I should have
known that there was nothing strange in the way
in which that mind and heart were being moved
and drawn to higher things. I should have known
that God was allowing the winds to blow for a
little while, allowing the tempests to sweep for a
little space across that yearning soul; that, presently, in all the plenitude of the love which is as
sweet as it is infinite; in all the abundance of the
mercy which is as patient as it is without measure, He might come moving across the troubled
waters, and bid the angry winds and waves be
still; might bring, in all their plenitude, light, and
peace, and rest to the heart that had sought for
them so simply and so truly, and which found at
last that which it had sought; found it in a plen-
tifulness and a profusion far beyond its fondest
hopes, far beyond its wildest expectations; found
it in a measure which flows but from one hand
alone, and that the loving hand of a loving God,
of a God whose tender mercies are above all his
works.

Yes, if I had known God, and the ways of God,
I should have understood all these things. As it
was, in my foolishness and my ignorant self-suffi-

ciency, I only thought them *very strange*, strange, indeed, far beyond my comprehension!

As his thoughts grew clearer, and his ideas more developed, so did he express himself to me with more definiteness and precision on the few occasions on which we spoke on religious matters. When we had been some time at Oxford he came across one of the most remarkable men of the day, a man whose intellect was critical and deep, whilst it was daring almost to rashness; a man whose opinions in regard to many most important and essential points of doctrine and belief were far in advance of those of, perhaps, any other man of his day; a man who, whilst he indubitably raised many doubts in their minds, and set many earnest men thinking on matters which should, from their nature, and which, in reality, did lead them into the bosom of God's holy Catholic Church, died himself, in the inscrutable designs of Divine Providence, a weary wanderer outside the saving gates, whose portals his earnest burning words had caused so many burthened souls to seek and to find to their everlasting gain. This extraordinary man had a wonderful influence upon the youth who hung upon his words, and drank in with such earnest enthusiasm the views and the opinions, which were so powerfully conceived and so vividly expressed, concerning the constitution of the Church of God, its hierarchical system, and the dignity and power of its priesthood. He expressed in sharp, clear,

precise words his conviction of the existence of a
fixed, defined, unchangeable body of doctrine
which the Church of Christ alone had been commissioned to teach,—ideas which had been the
dream, nay, rather let me say the desire and the
hope of my friend's early years, his years of doubt
and uncertainty; and which were now unfolded
to him for the first time in the earnest language
of a logical, ardent, and truly sincere man; a man
who believed what he said, and who practised
what he believed; a man who could no more be
satisfied with the uncertain and wavering belief,
the dreamy, chilling creed and practice of Protestantism, than an angel can be satisfied with anything less than God; than the craving, yearning
heart of man can be satisfied with anything less
than the possession of that perfect happiness for
which it has been created. This great and, as I
believe, good man was full of high and holy
thoughts, full of tender reverent ideas of the saints
of God, and, most of all, of the Blessed Virgin
Mary. He entertained views which, I think, were
nearly, if not entirely Catholic, in regard to positive sanctity, and the possibility of attaining it;
whilst he as truly looked upon the practice of
penance and self-denial, both external and internal, as the means of arriving at its heights. What,
perhaps, was more striking than all the rest, he
had a firm faith and belief in the Real Presence
of Christ in the sacrament of the altar. I have

only mentioned some points, but there were others of vital importance on which his views were no less clear, no less pronounced. He was not a man to hide within his own breast what, in his heart of hearts, he held to be God's everlasting truth; and, therefore, he spoke and taught as boldly as he believed deeply. When I have said that this man with his clear, definite ideas, and his earnest, burning words, had a wonderful influence upon Eustace Percy, I have expressed but very feebly what I wish to say. It was more than influence: it was positive action, the wonderful mysterious action of one soul upon another which is understood when it is felt, but which, I think, can never be described; which I, at all events, am not able to describe. I as little express what I mean when I say that Eustace hung upon his lips, and drank in his words, as eagerly as the hunted stag drinks at the cooling lake, before he plunges into it as his last chance for life. I think, too, that the earnest, ardent man who found so few prepared to give assent to his teaching, fewer still to follow his teachings to their legitimate deductions and conclusions, was proud of the enthusiastic youth who was such a willing, nay, even, a longing listener to him; who yielded such a ready assent to the opinions which he advanced; who reduced to practice so simply, and with such child-like docility, the principles of devotion and of sanctity which he proposed to him; and who, all the while,

made no secret of his love, his admiration, and his
reverence for his teacher. At all events, whilst I
am pretty sure that the gifted, winning man, of
whom I have said, perhaps, more than enough to
enable any of his contemporaries who may chance
to read these lines to recognize the portrait which
I have endeavoured to sketch, had no disciple, if
I may so call him, who was dearer to him, or in
whom he took a greater interest than Eustace
Percy, I am equally certain that on his death in
183—, there were few who regretted his loss more
deeply, or who shed more bitter tears over his
premature departure than my friend, who had first
heard from him those principles which, rightly
and simply applied, led him into the paths of
truth; and who grieved all the more deeply, all
the more sadly for his master and his friend, because *he*, as I have already said, died outside the
pale of the Church, died, as I humbly hope and
trust, in good faith, and in perfect sorrow for sin;
but whom, nevertheless, dying as he did, without
having been received into the bosom of her who
is alone the mother and the mistress of all the
churches, we are not able to regard and think of
with all that perfect confidence, that trusting
assurance which takes away the most bitter sting
from the death of those who die in the peace of
God, and the communion of his holy Catholic
Church.

As the influence of him, who was now the

teacher and the master of Eustace, grew every day more powerful over his disciple, I began to feel a nervous, undefined anxiety as to what must be the end of all this. I am free to admit, too, that no small degree of jealousy mixed itself up with this anxiety. Under the circumstances, as he was necessarily much in the rooms of his new friend, he was naturally less with me; and he was so dear above all price to me, I had been accustomed to such unreserved confidence from, as well as influence over him, that I resented bitterly the interference, as I considered it, of this later friend of his; and this, as well from my dread of the issue of that acquaintance, as on account of my own wounded and irritated feelings. Little as I knew, and less as I then cared, God forgive me, about what I considered merely matters of opinion, I had penetration enough to understand that these new ideas of which Eustace was so full must, of their own nature, lead him out of the beaten track, which I was walking with so much complacent satisfaction to myself, into other and what I deemed far more dangerous and slippery paths. Hence, loving him as I did, and sensitively alive as I was to everything which concerned him, even in the most distant manner, I was almost as angry with Eustace for allowing himself, as I thought, to be thus led astray into dangerous paths, as I was indignant with him who thus, as it appeared to me, practised upon the ardent and enthusiastic nature of my friend. For a little while, but only for a little while, a shadow came between me and my friend. He was ever the same to me; there was no change in him; but I, do as I would, and I struggled hard with my touchy, sensitive pride, could not help showing some little irritation and soreness of mind and heart, some little constraint towards him with whom I had always hitherto been on such terms of cordial, open, unreserved friendship. He very soon noticed it, and one day when, being in worse humour and more irritated than usual, I answered him crossly, almost sharply, the hot blood rushed in an instant to his face, from which, however, it passed as quickly away, whilst I saw the tears start to his eyes at such strange and unusual conduct on my part. At another time I should have been utterly and completely ashamed of myself, and should have been begging his pardon almost before the words had left my lips; but, as it was, I experienced a kind of a malignant satisfaction in seeing that I had made him understand how deeply I felt, and how bitterly I resented his conduct and mode of action towards me; and, although I think it was the first time, as I am quite certain that it was the last, on which I ever wilfully or intentionally brought one tear of sorrow to *his* eye, I stood aloof in the bitterness of my wounded pride, and made no effort to excuse myself to him, or soothe the pain which my harsh and angry words had caused him.

A moment more and he was at my side. "Ambrose," I heard him say, in tones in which surprise and astonishment were mingled with emotion and pain, "Ambrose, what is the matter? why do you look so strangely at me, and speak such cold, harsh words to me? what have I done to you? how have I offended you? for, indeed, indeed, I am not conscious of having deserved such words from you as those which you have just spoken to me. What is it, my friend; Ambrose, my oldest friend, what is it? Only tell me what I have done to you, only let me know how I have offended you."

He spoke in hurried words, with a voice which so often had moved my soul to its very depths, but for the moment my pride hardened my heart against him, as I turned away my head and answered him never a word. For a few moments the room was still as death, as I sat knitting my brows, and gazing gloomily out of the opposite window, and hardening my heart still more and more against him—him who was so infinitely my superior in everything that was pure and true. Then a little while, and I felt the hand that rested on my shoulder tremble. A moment more, and several scalding tears had fallen on my brow, and rolled along my cheeks, and then, with one great start, I sprang to my feet, and tried to stammer out some eager, pleading words with which I begged his pardon from the bottom of my heart, with which I prayed him to forget and forgive me all my testy pride, my surly anger, my harsh and bitter words to him whom I loved and prized above all other of my earthly friends. For several minutes he did not speak to me, but at last he took my hand, and then I knew that he had forgiven me. I knew that the shadow had passed away. I knew that my friend and I were one again in a union of love and truth, never to be broken more, at least by word or act of mine.

"You know, Eustace," I stammered out at last, "you know I acted as I did towards you simply because I loved you so much. It has seemed to me for the last few weeks as if you had less confidence in me, almost as if you had less friendship for me. I have seen you," and here some portion of the old jealousy broke out again, "I have seen you bestowing your confidences elsewhere, and the sight has been so bitter to me that it was more than I could do, although I have striven hard, to keep my spite, my vexation, and my wounded feelings to myself, and to-day they have escaped me in a way which makes me disgusted with myself and ashamed to look you in the face. Of course you are at liberty to act as you like. I may think that you will never find a truer friend than him whom you have known so long, but I have as little right as I have inclination to dictate to you where your confidences are to be reposed, or your friendship bestowed. I am sorry that I offended you, Eustace," I concluded, and, do as I would, there was some of the old hardness and bitterness in my tones; " I am sorry that I offended you by my thoughtless and unfeeling words, and I beg your pardon with all my heart and soul."

As I went on I had marked an expression of surprise and pain passing across his face; and before he answered me he looked at me long and earnestly, as if he scarcely comprehended my meaning, or as if he could scarcely persuade himself that I was sincere in what I was saying. When at length he spoke to me, it was with a voice unusually full of emotion, even for him, " I see it all, Ambrose," he said, " my dear old fellow, I see it all. I have pained you because I am so much with ——, because I seem to place so much confidence in him. He's a glorious fellow," continued Eustace, with a flush of enthusiasm upon his face; " but, Ambrose, my dear old Ambrose, surely you don't believe or think that he can ever be the same to me that you are. You know," he went on, his face kindling more and more, " you know that he has been a great help to me in many ways, and I admire him very much. I believe in him with all my heart, and I love him, too; but not in the same way, you know, in which I love you. I trust in him much, but, you know, I can never trust in any other man as I love and trust in you. I thought you would have known and felt all this," he added, with the slightest tinge of sadness in his voice, " or I would have spoken to you about it long ago. I know that you don't care much about these matters which are so interesting to me, and which —— explains to me as I never heard them explained before; and this is the only reason why I did not speak more to you upon this subject. I didn't want to bore or annoy you," he continued, " but if I had ever dreamt that you could have misunderstood me so far as you have done, I would have taken good care, no matter how I might have pestered you, to have explained all these things to you. I can't afford to lose *you*, Ambrose," he went on, his voice sinking to a whisper, and his hand trembling more and more as it rested on mine, " I can't afford to lose *you*. God only knows what the future has in store for me, and I can't afford to lose you—I can't afford to lose you."

He repeated these words so often, and in such a sad tone of voice, that, despite my efforts to restrain them, several tears forced their way from my eyes, and one of them rolled down upon his hand. As he felt it, I saw him look with astonishment at the little drop as it rested where it fell, for it was but seldom that a tear made its way from my eye. I was affected more than I liked to admit, even to myself, by his words; and that strange presentiment of evil, which I had first experienced during my visit to Percy Grange, came over me again a thousand times stronger and more powerfully than ever. As soon as I had mastered the emotion which his words had produced in me, I ventured to speak to him of the future at which he had thus hinted. In all the earnestness of my love for him I begged and besought of him to consider whether he was not entering on dangerous paths, whether he was not preparing a future for himself which might be one of misery and of pain, whether it would not be better for him to stop short at once and make himself contented with things as they were. Most of all, I begged him to consider whether he in whom he trusted so much, and to whom he looked up with such implicit credence, were either a safe or a prudent guide in matters such as those of which we spoke.

When he raised his eyes to mine, ere he answered me, they were all on fire with confidence and trust in me, with enthusiastic feeling and interest in the subject which was so near and dear to him.

"I cannot go back, Ambrose," he said; "God is leading me, I know not whither, and I scarcely know how; but, God is surely leading me, and I cannot go back. Neither can I think," he went on, "that —— is a dangerous or an unsafe guide. I knew nothing. I had no fixed ideas, it was all mist, and darkness, and perplexity till I met him, and I cannot believe that one who has given such definiteness to my belief, one who has taught me so much that is good and holy, can be leading me astray. Where it may end, or what the future may have in store for me I cannot tell, I cannot foresee. The shadow that I told you of," he cried, sinking his voice to a whisper so low that I could scarcely catch its tones, " seems to be drawing nearer, nearer, nearer to me; and, sometimes, it chills me with a dread that freezes me to my very heart; but, oh! Ambrose, Ambrose," he added, trembling till I could scarcely hold him, " whatever that future may be, I *cannot* go back. God is leading me, and I cannot and I dare not turn back. Oh, anything but that—anything but turning back!"

Again, he turned away his head and sobbed a little while; not with sobs, soft and gentle as the summer's falling rain, but sobs which seemed to force their way out of a heart that was suffering mortal throes, sobs that seemed as if they would choke him as they rose gurgling in his throat. Presently, however, he came to, and spoke to me once more. "Ambrose," he said, "I have two favours to ask of you. Say that you will grant me my requests." I pressed his hand in silence, and he went on. "Promise me, then," he said, "that you will come to my rooms to-night and meet ——, or else I shall not believe that you have completely banished your jealousy from your heart." It went rather against the grain to do it, but, nevertheless, I promised him at once what he asked of me. At the moment I would have done much more to show my penitence and my remorse for the unworthy doubts which I had so lately entertained of his friendship and truth.

After I had promised him this he rose to his feet, and, I, instinctively did the same. He came close to me and took both my hands in his, and looked into my eyes with a strangely earnest and imploring look. He gazed at me thus for a moment or two ere he attempted to speak to me. At last he bent his head down to my ear, and whispered to me out of the fulness of his simple heart, "Oh, Ambrose, dear Ambrose, promise me, too, that *you* will never forsake me. Promise me that, whatever the future may have in store for me, it shall never separate me from you. Promise me that you will never think less well of me; tell me that I may reckon for evermore upon your faithful friendship, your faithful, never-failing help. Let me think that I shall have at least one heart to lean upon, if the troubles which I dread so much shall fall upon me. Oh, Ambrose, promise me this—oh, promise me this."

It is not in mere words that promises such as that which I was called upon to make are made; but, nevertheless, I managed to find some with which I promised him what he sought of me; promised him that nothing which might ever happen to him should suffice to separate him from me, to make me love him one whit the less deeply or the less truly. I told him that, whilst the sky was fair and the clouds were bright, he might wander where he listed, and that I would never doubt him again, never again question his fidelity or his truth. But, most of all, I told and bade him remember that, if the clouds should darken and the storms should gather, this was the time he would ever be most dear to the heart whose friendship he so truly prized, prized, indeed, far above its worth, the heart which called God to witness with what earnest, hearty, simple faith it was ready to shed the last drop of its blood to shield him, as far as might be, from one moment of sorrow and of pain.

CHAPTER VII.

ON THE BRINK.

I KEPT my promise to him, and that evening I went to his rooms to meet ——, whom, as yet, I did not personally know. When I arrived, I found already assembled not only him whom Eustace had especially asked me to meet, but also several of the heads of that great party of which —— was certainly one of the chiefs. I was introduced to them, for, up to this time, I had never spoken to any of them; although, of course, I had heard a good deal about them, and the strange and dangerous doctrines which they were already broaching in conversation, and even in their pulpits; and which, later on, they put forward so much more definitely and precisely through the medium of the " British Magazine," the " British Critic," and the famous " Tracts for the Times." They struck me as singularly earnest and sincere men, but, nevertheless, I didn't like them. Perhaps it would be more correct if I said that I was afraid of them, and all the more afraid, because I could as little comprehend and understand, as I could then appreciate and value them. I need

scarcely say that nearly the whole conversation of
the evening was on religious topics, and, especially,
on those subjects which were then agitating the
minds of so many other thinking men in Oxford,
besides those who were assembled in the rooms of
my friend. I was greatly puzzled by the talk
which went on around me; and the more I heard
the more I was puzzled, and the more I was convinced that these men, although I could not doubt
their sincerity, were very dangerous companions;
for, whilst they were continually speaking of the
Roman Church as being filled with the spirit of
Antichrist, as being anti-Christian, and a great
deal more to the same effect, they were as continually preaching up and defending doctrines and
practices which, so far as I knew, were only held
and practised in the same Roman Church. When,
however, anything more violent than usual was
said against Rome, —— always rushed impetuously to its defence, and, making no secret of his
open admiration for the Roman Church, retorted
upon its assailants by some fierce attack upon the
Reformers. Spite of his warm language and his
advocacy of principles which sounded so strange
to me, I felt more inclined to love him than any
of his companions, whilst, at the same time, I became more and more convinced in my own mind
that he was a very dangerous man, and one who
would surely lead, if he had not already led, my
friend, Eustace Percy, very far astray. We were

assembled ostensibly for a wine party, but I think there was very little drank during the evening, whilst the continual and ready flow of conversation on subjects which appeared to me dry and abstruse, beyond all comprehension, completely bewildered me; and I felt quite relieved when the party had broken up, and I and Eustace were left to enjoy a quiet hours' chat by ourselves. He had been in great spirits the whole evening, and it had pained me more than I can well say to see how eagerly he listened to the discussions which went on, what open admiration he showed for ——, and with what earnestness he drank in every word which fell from the lips of that truly dangerous man, as I could not help considering him. After the scene which had taken place between us no later than that very morning, I did not like, terribly anxious as I felt about him, to introduce the subject again; but Eustace soon relieved me from my difficulty on this head by commencing it himself. In fact, he was so full of it that I think it was a kind of necessity for him to speak about it, and he began the conversation abruptly by asking me my opinion of ——.

"Tell me, candidly, what you think of him, Ambrose," he began; "your candid and unprejudiced opinion, you know," he added, archly. "Isn't he a glorious fellow, now? Did you ever hear such great views as he has? Did you ever hear a man who could express his views in such grand and truthful terms; who could bring before you in such a forcible way all that he wishes to say, all that he wishes to persuade you to accept? Tell the truth, now, isn't he a glorious fellow?"

I think I shrugged my shoulders, and made a wry face or two before I answered. "I don't deny," I said at last, somewhat coldly, "that he seems to be a very earnest and sincere man. Nay," I added, as I saw a look of disappointment flit across the face of my friend, "I am quite ready to admit, if you like, that he *is* a glorious fellow; but then, Eustace, my dear friend," I continued, as earnestly as ever I could, "a man may be a very glorious fellow, and yet may be a very dangerous companion or a very unsafe guide, and I am very much afraid that this new friend of yours" (the old bitterness again) "is both the one and the other. I am very much afraid that you don't see whither he is leading you, whilst it is very obvious to me that he is certainly leading you into paths which are as dangerous in themselves as they can be productive of nothing but misery to you and all who love you; and I should not be doing my duty to you as a friend if I did not tell you what I think on these matters, although I am quite sure that you are much better able to instruct me on such questions than I am you. Still, ignorant as I may be on those topics, which your friends discussed so eagerly and with such profundity of argument this evening, I have knowledge enough, I hope, to see that they are dangerous ones, and that they are opposed to that simple gospel truth which has been quite sufficient to guide better men than we are to their rest in God, and which, therefore, ought to be quite sufficient for us, too, without entangling ourselves with these new-fangled notions which have been unheard of till now." Of course I had no particular meaning when I spoke of " simple gospel truth," but it was a sentence which I had heard repeated so continually that, without attaching any particular signification to it, I had taken it up as a very expressive and very Christian-like phrase, and I now threw it at Eustace as a "clincher" which must settle him at once. Of course, if these new ideas, of which he was so full, were, of their nature and essentially, opposed to the simplicity of gospel truth, there could be no more said about it. He must give them up at once. Therefore, with that ready assurance, which is so useful in disputation, and which, if it only be employed with sufficient boldness, will make up for the want of any amount of argument and truth; I unflinchingly asserted, first, that these ideas which had taken possession of my friend's mind were *new;* and, secondly, that they were opposed essentially to the simplicity of gospel truth. I had never heard of them before; *ergo*, I concluded that they were new. The curate of Atherby had never said anything about them in his sermons, so far as I recollected; *ergo*, they were opposed to the simplicity of gospel truth. *O tempora! O mores!* What logic! All that I have to say for it is that I don't attempt to defend it, although I employed it with a great deal of satisfaction to myself, and confidence in my cause, on this memorable occasion.

As I laid down this "clinching" argument of mine, poor Eustace looked at me half sorrowfully, and yet with an expression that had almost as much of good-humoured amazement as of regret in it. "Why, you ridiculous old-fellow," he said, "I'm quite ashamed of you. Because I have begun to get a little light upon certain matters, and to have some understanding of that which God expects from me, you take fright all at once and protest that I am off full gallop along paths which must lead me to destruction. You know well, Ambrose, no one knows so well as you do, the miserable state I was in when I left Atherby school. You know that I had no belief, that is, that I had no fixed ideas on anything connected with God and the salvation of my soul. I didn't know what to believe, and what not to believe. You know, as well as I do, that I was 'tossed to and fro, and carried about with every wind of doctrine,' although, indeed, I must say," he continued, "that my acquaintance with doctrine of any kind was on a very limited scale; and, you know, too," he went on, growing very earnest and very enthusiastic, " that this was through no fault of mine. You know that I always wished to do my duty to God, and that I always believed in my heart that God must have laid down somewhere or other, in clear, precise terms, what I was bound to believe, and what I was bound to practise; and, yet, I could never make it out. Not as I have just said through any fault of mine, but through the fault of the system which never taught me better; which never laid down in clear terms what I must necessarily believe; which never told me, except in the most vague, general, and unmeaning manner, what virtues I must necessarily practise. You know, too, how nearly I was driven by all this into indifferentism and sin: and then, because when I come here, and happen to meet with a zealous, sincere, learned man, who shows me that God *did* intend me to have a fixed unwavering belief, that God did leave a body of doctrine for my guidance and as the ground of my faith, I listen to him with pleasure, I give my assent willingly and cheerfully to what I cannot doubt, you take alarm and cry out that I am on dangerous paths, that I am drifting away, nobody knows where, as nobody can tell how; that I am lost, and all the rest of it." He was going on, but at this point I interrupted him with another " clinching argument," one which I thought he would never be able to get over, although he had made so little of my last one.

"I don't quarrel with you, Eustace, my dear fellow, I surely don't quarrel with you," I said, " for wishing to see your way as clearly as possible. I may think that you wish to see things which God never intended you to see. I may think that you wish to walk open-eyed, whilst God wishes you to walk by faith. I may think that you, in your earnestness and good faith, which I can no more question that I can question the fact of my own existence, are desirous of putting limits to Christian liberty which God never intended to put upon it. I may think a great deal more to the same effect; but I can never be so foolish or so inconsistent as to wish to prevent you from investigating these momentous questions to the utmost of your power, provided this investigation be carried on in a safe and proper way; but where I quarrel with you, and where I see the danger which threatens you, is, that, instead of seeking for God's truth where He alone intended you to seek it, viz., in His holy Word, you are relying upon miserable men like yourself, you are relying upon the teaching of man rather than the teaching of God, you are neglecting or throwing over your Bible in order that you may listen to the vain theories of, it may be sincere, but certainly, weak, fallible mortals like yourself; theories which, so far as I have heard and can comprehend them, are either full of novelty, or bordering upon the errors of that Church which you and I, Eustace, have always been taught to consider as false and corrupt. This is where I quarrel with you. This is where I believe you to be grievously astray. This is where the danger which I fear so much is hidden, the danger, which, I pray God, may exist in my imagination alone."

"Well, Ambrose," he answered, "although we won't go into that question just at present, you know it doesn't necessarily follow that the Church of Rome is false and corrupt because you and I have been taught to consider her such; and I am by no means certain that the teachers we have had up to this have been either very competent to give an opinion on this matter, or, that their opinion, when given, has been worth very much." It pained me more than ever to hear him speak in this way, because it was only now that I perceived how deeply he was tainted, as I considered, and how firm a hold the views of this new friend and teacher of his had taken on him. Still, I did not interrupt him, and he went on. "Yes," he resumed, "we won't speak at present of the claims of the Church of Rome to be considered as a branch, more or less pure, of the Church of Christ; but you must pardon me, dear old fellow, if I can't at all agree with you as to the reasonableness of taking the holy Scriptures, interpreted according to my own will and fancy, as my sole rule of faith. Nay," he continued, as he saw the expression of amazement and pain which these words of his, so new, and so dangerous and wicked, as they appeared to me, caused to pass across my face,—" Nay, I may as well be very frank with you, Ambrose, as we are on this subject, and I confess to you, openly and freely, that I don't believe that the sacred Scriptures, interpreted according to the fancy of each individual, constitute that supreme judge in all matters of faith which must necessarily exist in the Church of God, any more than I believe the sacred Scriptures, thus interpreted, to be either a safe, or a sufficient rule of faith. I am certain that there must be in the Church some supreme authority, competent and appointed by God, to decide all matters of faith and belief. I am equally certain that this supreme authority must be obvious; so that all men may easily have recourse to it, and that no one may be able to allege that he had no means of solving his doubts. It must be clear; there must be no doubt, no hesitation, no obscurity in its decisions, otherwise it could not attain its end, viz., unity of faith, and the removing of all doubts from the minds of believers. It must be common to all; for if there were any professing Christians who were not subject to its authority, they could, of course, reject its decisions, and hence, again, it would not attain its end—unity of faith. Above all, and before all, it must necessarily be infallible; because, whatever is defined by this supreme judge becomes the object of faith, and it is absurd to suppose that anything can thus be an object of faith, if the authority which defines and presents it to us, is not to be considered as infallible. I am quite sure," he repeated, "that there does exist in the Church such a supreme judge of controversy, and I am equally sure that it is not in the holy Scriptures, interpreted according to your whim or mine, that we are to look for it. But, you don't seem to follow me, Ambrose," he said, as he saw me turn away my head to hide the annoyance which I felt, and which I could not help showing at his words: "you don't seem to follow me."

"Oh, yes, I follow you well enough, Eustace," I answered, bitterly; "I follow you well enough. I didn't know that you were so advanced in your new theories as to have thrown God's Word overboard, but, now, that you have got so far as this, of course I shall not be astonished at anything that may follow. Only, you see, I am taken aback and I can't realize it all at once, but I follow you well enough, nevertheless. I understand that you begin by rejecting God's holy Word—I see this plainly enough—I wish that I could only see the end as clearly as I see the beginning——."

He took me up quickly in his earnest, ardent way before I could say more. "Why, you illogical and inconsistent fellow," he said, "how can you talk such nonsense! I throw God's blessed Word overboard, as you express it! I reject God's

Word! God forbid that I should do anything so wicked or so unchristian. But, what right have you to accuse me of such a thing?" he went on; "what right have you to accuse me of rejecting the sacred Scriptures because I tell you that I do not believe the Bible alone to be a complete and precise rule of faith. I admit with all my heart, I believe quite as firmly as you can possibly do, that the holy Scriptures have been inspired by God. I believe that the Bible is the most holy and the most wonderful book in the world; a book worthy of all reverence, all love, and all veneration; but, whilst admitting all this most freely, most unreservedly, I do not believe that the Bible is the Christian's only rule of faith, and this, because I am certain that God never *intended* it to be. Now, don't get into a passion," he went on, "but listen to me quietly for a few moments till I explain what I mean. I think you won't venture to contradict St. Paul, when he tells you that the end and the object of all Christian teaching is unity of faith, a knowledge of the Son of God, and a firm stability in the apprehension of all Christian doctrine necessary to eternal salvation. You know that it was precisely to secure this object that Christ our Lord, before He ascended to His Father, constituted and appointed various grades of pastors and teachers—some apostles, and some prophets, and other some evangelists, and other some pastors and doctors. . . . .

for the perfecting of the saints, for the work of the ministry, for the edifying of the body of Christ, until we all meet into *the unity of faith*, and of the knowledge of the Son of God. . . . . That henceforth we be no more children, tossed to and fro, and carried about by every wind of doctrine, &c. (Ephes. 4th chap.). Now, if one of the ends of all Christian teaching be unity of faith, and if this unity of faith be an essential mark and condition, as it is, of the true Church of Christ, it necessarily follows that there must be some rule of faith which will secure this necessary unity, some supreme tribunal which will decide upon those points of controversy which, considering the nature of man, will from time to time arise; which will decide with a final and infallible judgment what is, or what is not, the object of a Christian's faith. I say, moreover, that any system of teaching which tends of its nature and very essence to destroy this unity of faith; to unsettle men's minds on the most serious and momentous questions, as, for example, belief in the divinity of the Son of God; which, after long years of fair trial, years during which it has had every possible advantage on its side, leaves its supporters and disciples tossed to and fro with every wind of doctrine in the fullest sense of the word, is a false and a rotten system, and such a system I, from my heart, believe to be that which teaches that the Bible, and the Bible alone, the Bible interpreted according to each one's own view of its meaning, is the Christian's complete, exact, and only rule of faith. And look at the history of the last 300 years," he went on, before I could interpose or put in a word. " Look at the effects which have followed, legitimately enough, from the principle that each one has a right to read the Bible for himself, has a right to be his own interpreter, has a right to make his Bible, thus read and thus interpreted, his sole and only rule of faith. I won't stop now to consider," he continued, " the absurdity of supposing that every illiterate cobbler who takes up his Bible is able to understand those passages, which St. Peter himself tells us " are difficult to be understood, and which the unlearned and unstable wrest, as they do also the other Scriptures, to their own destruction" (St. Peter, 2nd Epis., 3rd ch., 16th verse). Neither will I stop to ask how you, or even the most learned man in this university, can be certain that he possesses the Scriptures as they were left by their inspired writers; and, yet, if the Bible and the Bible alone is to be your rule of faith, you must be certain of this. If you are faithful to your principles, you ought, *by your own examination*, to make yourself certain of the fidelity and truth of the different versions; and, as they were originally written in the Greek and Hebrew tongues, you should be a perfect master of these languages. Having satisfied yourself of the fidelity of the version, you must then determine for yourself the genuine sense of those passages which have puzzled and perplexed the most acute intellects which the world ever saw. I will not ask you what you will say to me when I remind you that for many hundred years the Roman Church, which you have just told me is so false and corrupt, was the only guardian of the sacred writings; when I ask you how you know, what certainty you have, that she did not corrupt and change even the most essential passages? Of course, I don't mean to say that she did. I don't mean to attach much weight to this argument; but, how will you prove to me strictly and conclusively, and, above all, of *your own positive knowledge*, that she did not do so? But if you once admit authority, if you once admit the testimony of man, you are forsaking your first principles, principles which, my dear fellow, however much you may profess to believe in them, neither you nor any other sane man ever thinks of acting upon. Still, if you are to be a consistent man, you must prove all these things for yourself, and by yourself, before you can take the Bible and the Bible alone for your rule of faith. Neither will I stop to ask you," he continued, " how those who are utterly unable to read their Bible, and those who are unable to understand anything but what is put before them in the most simple and familiar way, but who, nevertheless, have immortal souls to be saved, souls which are as precious in the sight of God as either yours or mine, are to find *their* rule of faith in the Bible and the Bible alone! I will not stop to ask you how such men as these, ignorant, stupid, illiterate men, who, after all, form the greater portion of mankind, are to extract for themselves from a Bible which they cannot even read, those saving and essential truths the knowledge of which is so absolutely necessary to salvation, that no amount of ignorance will render the absence of it excusable in the sight of God! No, Ambrose, I will not stop to discuss any of these points, which are more or less theoretical, with you. Only be sure, my friend," he added, in tones of deep and earnest conviction, "that God never intended man to be led to his end by any such a system as this. Even supposing for a moment, that it might suffice to direct you and me, of what possible use or assistance could it be to those who not only do not possess our knowledge and information, but who are utterly unlearned? and yet I never heard that there was one way to heaven for them, and another for us. I think we must all travel by the one, obvious, clear, common, and infallible path; the path which in His infinite goodness and loving mercy God has provided for us all, the path which is as secure and as safe, as clear and as obvious to the poor beggar who sits by the door of the church, and travels along to his rest by the road of suffering and of pain, as it is to the Doctor in the pulpit inside, who, whilst he can with ease explain and settle for you the most abstract questions in theology, explain to you with the masterly skill of the trained intellect and the ready tongue, the reasonableness and the motives of the faith that is in him, is only too happy to submit in his turn that intellect to the guidance of the authority which God has placed over him, only too happy to walk in all simplicity, in all docility, and meekness, along that path which he has so clearly and so convincingly pointed out to others. No, I will ask you none of these things, but let us leave for a while mere questions of theory, and let us come to facts. This rule of faith which takes the Bible, and the Bible alone, for its motto, has surely had full scope for all legitimate development during the last 300 years, and what effect has it produced? What have been its results? Why, such disunions and enmities on matters of religion as the world never saw before,—as are a positive scandal and reproach. There is scarcely a dogma of Christian truth which has not been called in question, and denied by some sect or other. And, yet, all their differences are grounded upon, and defended by, the interpretation of the same Bible. Each sect, or each individual, starts from the same principle, the private interpretation of the Scriptures; but, what one man asserts to be in the Bible, another protests as confidently is not to be found there; and who is to judge between them? There is no way of bringing them to a unity of faith; for he who denies the presence of any particular doctrine in the Bible, has just as much right to his opinion as he who asserts the very opposite. They have both the same right to read the Scripture for themselves, and to take their own meaning out of it. One has as much right to be considered conscientious and sincere as the other. One is as infallible as the other; and the end of it all is, that they form contradictory opinions upon the most momentous questions, from their private interpretation of the same Bible; and, as they acknowledge no higher authority in such matters than their own judgment, there is no possible way of reducing them to that unity of faith which, as I have already said, I believe to be the end of all Christian teaching, as I believe it to be an essential quality of the Church of Christ. Religious disagreement and heresy are the natural and essential results of such a system," he added, vehemently; " and I will never believe that it came from God, that it has the sanction and the blessing of God, any more than I will believe that God ever intended any man to be guided to his end through its means. No, I cannot, and I will not believe it!"

"But, Eustace," I rejoined, interrupting him sharply, for I was thoroughly angry and annoyed to hear him talk in what I naturally considered such a wild way, "Eustace, in your unbecoming anxiety to throw dirt on God's Word—an anxiety which I as little expected to see in you, as it pains me when I do thus see it, you forget that these differences, of which you make so much, are in no way 'fundamental,' that they in no way regard the essential points of Christian belief, that they are merely such as must exist amongst men whose judgment is essentially fallible; men to whom God, in very consideration of this fallibility, has granted the glorious privilege of Christian liberty, and from whom he expects no such absolute unity of belief as that which you have spoken so much about. You either forget, or you ignore this altogether; and I think if those from whom you are deriving such new views," I added, bitterly, " had enlightened you a little more on this point, it would have been vastly better both for you and for themselves."

"Oh, well, now, Ambrose," he answered, "if you are going to get into a passion about it, we will say no more on the subject. I don't see any reason why we should quarrel; and if we cannot discuss this matter quietly, we won't discuss it at all."

He looked at me so earnestly and affectionately, as he uttered these words, that spite of my annoyance, I could not help smiling at him, and bidding him proceed, and that I would take care to keep myself quite cool and placid, no matter what strange or horrible things he might say.

"But, first of all," he resumed, "I must protest

against your saying, my dear old fellow, that I am anxious to throw dirt on God's Word. I know you didn't mean it ; but it's a very strong remark, more forcible, indeed, than elegant, and I must insist upon your immediate retractation. I tell you," he added earnestly, " as I told you before, that I prize and esteem and revere God's holy and inspired Word, quite as highly as you or any other man in the world can possibly do. Indeed, my esteem and reverence for it is such, that this is one of the great reasons why I cannot bear to see it abused as it is. I cannot bear to see every tinker twisting and turning it to suit his own meaning, and pretending to find doctrines contained in it which certainly never came from God ; and which, for anything I know, came from a very different quarter."

He was going on, but at this juncture, I called him to order, and requested to know who was losing his temper now, and whether it would not be as well to keep the tinker alluded to, as much as possible in his natural sphere, which was, probably, one of modest retirement—one of tins and kettles, rather than of polemical disputation. He laughingly acknowledged the call to order, and resumed.

"You ask me to remember," he continued, " that these differences of opinion of which I spoke are not fundamental or essential. Now, how can you talk such nonsense? Don't get vexed, old fellow," he added, " don't get vexed, whatever you do. And, in truth, it was very hard to get vexed with him. "But you *know* it's nonsense. I never heard that the Primitive Church taught that some articles of Christian faith were fundamental, whilst others were not fundamental. You know, as well as I do, that this distinction is a mere modern invention, the artifice by which a clever man endeavoured to wriggle himself out of a difficulty, which he saw clearly enough was unanswerable. You know equally well that this distinction rests on no foundation, and that it is utterly impossible to reduce it to practice. If these differences of opinion, of which we were speaking," he went on, "are not, as you say, to be considered essential, how is it that they have always been regarded as such by those who have held them? Why, you know well enough that many conscientious men have exposed themselves willingly and cheerfully to exile, imprisonment, social disabilities of every kind, loss of goods, fortune, and even of life itself, on account of those very principles, those matters of belief, which you say are not essential; but, do you think for a moment that these men would have suffered such grievous inconveniences in order to maintain these principles if they had not considered them to be essential? The supposition is absurd. There is no doubt that the Protestant non-conformists, of every shade of opinion, have considered those differences of belief, on which they have separated from the Church of England, and for which some

of them have suffered so much, as essential, and
who is to say that they are wrong? They find
their opinions in the Bible, just as you find the
contrary, and who is to judge between you?
But," he continued, growing warmer and warmer,
"let us come to these opinions themselves. Do
you hold the divinity of the Son of God to be an
essential portion of your belief? he suddenly asked
me. "Certainly," I answered, quickly; "how
can it be questioned?" "And, yet, you know quite
well," he rejoined, "that a large and respectable
body of professing Christians altogether reject
that doctrine, and maintain that it can neither be
proved nor held. What do you say to that?"
The real truth was, that I scarcely knew what
to say, but I stammered out something to the
effect that they were heretics; but the words were
scarcely out of my mouth before he took me up
again." "Heretics? Who shall say that they are
heretics? What right have you to say it? They
read their Bible for themselves, and they take
their own meaning out of it, and this is the meaning which they conscientiously and sincerely believe certain texts of Scripture to bear; and, yet,
you, who a moment ago held that these differences
of opinion were not on essential points, now cry
out heresy, rank, staring heresy! You call those
heretics who have just as much right as you have,
if you are only consistent to your principles, to
their opinion, because that opinion doesn't happen

to coincide with yours, Either such a difference
of opinion, my dear fellow, must be essential, or
you must be a very illiberal and inconsistent man,
which, you know, I'm not going to believe. Of
course, I might pursue the same line of argument
in regard to the satisfaction of Christ on the
cross, the necessity of baptism, and other doctrines which are positively denied by many,
whilst they are as firmly held by you and me, and
all who think as we do, to be absolutely essential;
but there is no need of it. No, let us confess the
truth, Ambrose—the unpleasant truth, if it must
be said—that this rule of faith of ours, instead
of leading us to that unity of belief which is so
essential to the Church of Christ, that unity which
should knit us so closely in the . . . " one body,
and one spirit . . . one Lord, one Faith, one
Baptism: one God and Father of all, who is above
all, and through all, and in us all," necessarily and
naturally leads even the most sincere and earnest
men to differences on points which no man can
consider unessential, unless he be prepared to
throw over the whole scheme of revelation and
redemption; leads them to deny, at one time or
another, every doctrine which has ever been held
by the Christian Church, with the exception, perhaps, of the mere existence of God, and we need
not go to the Scripture at all for that; the whole
world proclaims it to us; every bird that sings in
the summer sky, every flower that spreads its

petals to the sun, the whole world, and all that is in it, proclaims, with a never-ceasing voice, that the earth is the Lord's, and the fulness thereof; speaks to us of the divine hand which called them into existence, and which preserves them in all their living beauty, the hand whose works are all stamped with the same order and beautiful harmony, the same union and consistency in all their parts, and all their varied relations. No, let us be candid for once, and confess that such a system never came from the God, whose every work bears the impress of His own divine reason, His own infinite order and consistency. Let us never attempt to delude ourselves into the belief that our divine Lord himself laid down, and commissioned his apostles to make known to the world, those articles which he required us to believe, under pain of damnation, and then gave us such a system by which to arrive at the knowledge of those truths, as must, from its very nature, lead to inextricable confusion and doubt, as must necessarily destroy all certainty as to the deposit of revelation, and which, in fact, has led to the denial by sincere, but misguided and erring men, of those very articles which our Lord came upon earth to teach, if He came to teach anything. No, Ambrose, let us never believe anything so absurd as this. Let us not prate about Christian liberty on points of such awful and momentous importance as these."

He paused, and looked me in the face, as if to see what effect his words had produced upon me. He was so full of his subject, his eyes sparkled with such real enthusiasm, and his voice trembled with such deep earnestness, that I could not help listening to him, if not with pleasure, at least with a sort of attraction, which I could not shake off. That I did not listen to him with pleasure is certain, for I considered those views, which he expressed so fluently, and which had taken such a hold upon his keen and ardent nature, as unsound and dangerous in the extreme; but I scarcely knew what to say to him. It was the first time my attention had ever been seriously called to the point which we had been discussing; and, although I tried to hide it even from myself, I felt seriously disturbed and alarmed by what he had said to me; and this, not only on his account, but on my own. I had little doubt but that, with due time for reflection and inquiry, I should be able to answer all the difficulties which he had urged upon me; but, and there was no use in blinking it, at the moment I felt that I could not do so. I felt that I was on dangerous ground, and yet I had not knowledge and light enough to see where the danger was. I felt that he had thrown out principles which, unless I could refute them, must necessarily shake the very foundations of my religious belief, such as it was. Whether the light might ever come to me was more than I could say. All that I was sure of was, that, at present, I was groping in the dark, groping my way amongst pitfalls and snares, which were all the more dangerous, because they had been cast in my path by the hand of one whom I loved most deeply and most truly, one who was dearer to me than all the world besides, one whose words had an influence over me which was possessed by those of no other living man; an influence which tempted and inclined my heart to listen and believe, although my reason and my intellect rebelled against the principles which he laid down with such earnestness of feeling, and, above all, with such depth of conviction. No wonder, then, if I felt seriously disturbed and alarmed by the turn which our conversation had taken, and the phase which it had assumed; for, although I believed that I was honest enough to change my views, if I were once convinced that I ought to do so, I was sure that nothing was further from my heart than the desire of any change, and, least of all, a change in the direction which Eustace had taken, and to which his words seemed to impel me. However, I did my best to hide from him the uneasiness which his words had created in me. I strove to appear as if his arguments had produced no effect upon me.

"But, supposing you succeed, as you seem to propose to yourself," I retorted, "in destroying the authority of the holy Scriptures, what have you got to put in place of them? What do *you* propose as the rule of faith by which a Christian man is to be guided and directed in his search after divine truth? What have you got to give me that is more excellent, more holy, more immediately sprung from God, than the holy Scriptures, whose authority you are labouring so zealously to overturn? Will you tell me this?" I asked, both angrily and bitterly.

"Now, for the third time, Ambrose," he answered, good-humouredly, and taking no notice of my little display of temper, " for the third time I protest against your assertion that I am labouring to weaken and overthrow the authority of the sacred Scriptures. I am doing no such thing, and I have no such intention, as you know very well, and as I have already sufficiently explained to you. But, to pass over this, I will tell you what I believe, and what I hold, and what, to use your own words, which, however, I must remark, by the way, are very incorrect and badly put, I have to give you in place of the Scriptures. Instead of leaving every man, woman, and child to fish his own creed, according to his own taste or perverted judgment, out of the Scriptures, a system whose intrinsic absurdity, and whose obvious repugnance to the whole theory and idea of the Church, as it is laid before us in the inspired writings, I have sufficiently demonstrated to you, I believe that Christ left in His Church a divinely-commissioned body of teachers, whose duty it is, as well to guard from corruption, as to make known to the faithful, that code of doctrine which is contained, as well in the sacred Scriptures as in the deposit of tradition, and which He Himself made known to them, and commanded them to teach to all succeeding generations. I believe also that this body of teachers is authorized to decide all questions of doctrine and belief, and that it is infallible as well when it teaches, as when it decides on disputes or difficulties which may arise, from time to time, in the Church of Christ. I believe this body has the right to teach the highest and the most learned, just as much as the most lowly and the most ignorant. Taught, guided, and directed by it, I believe that the most humble and the most unlearned man upon the face of God's earth, is as secure of his salvation, is as certain that he holds precisely what God wishes and intends him to hold, as the most learned doctor, or the most profound theologian. Now, don't look so amazed, old fellow," he continued, " but just listen quietly whilst I give you my grounds for what, I dare say, appears a very strange, and, I suppose, you will add, a very dangerous opinion. I take up my Bible, and I find our divine Lord, at that very moment when He is about to ascend to His eternal Father, addressing some very solemn words to His disciples; words, which although I have often read,

I never fathomed or understood till lately: 'All power is given to Me in heaven and in earth . . . . going, therefore, teach ye all nations, teaching them to observe all things whatsoever I have commanded you, and, behold, I am with you all days, even to the consummation of the world. . . . He that believeth and is baptized, shall be saved; but he that believeth not shall be condemned." Now I am sure that our blessed Lord intended these most solemn words to have a real, a practical, and an obvious meaning; and, so far as I can see, and God knows how I have prayed that I might see their meaning," he went on, with an ever-growing and reverent earnestness which attracted me more and more, " they can have but one signification. I don't pretend to say that I come at it as logically and methodically as a trained theologian would do; but I come at it in my own way, nevertheless; and this is what I make of it. Our Lord begins by declaring that *all* power is given to Him in heaven and in earth; and that, having received it from His Father, by virtue of this same power He sends them, even as His eternal Father sent Him, to teach all nations, and to instruct them in those saving truths which are necessary for salvation; sends them in His own divine name, fortified with His own divine authority, to teach and enforce obedience to His lessons from those who are to be taught, declaring that those who despise the teachers whom He sends, despise Himself: 'He that despiseth you despiseth Me, and He that despiseth Me, despiseth Him that sent Me;' that it shall be more tolerable for Sodom and Gomorrah in the day of judgment than for that city, which will not receive and listen to those who have been appointed its teachers and guides in the way of salvation. And mind you, Ambrose, Christ speaks with this terrible emphasis only in favour of those whom He appointed, and their legitimate successors, those with whom He promised to be to the consummation of the world; not in favour of those who appoint themselves, who assume an office to which they were never called, and for which, under every point of view, many who do thus assume it, are so palpably unfit. The second conclusion which I draw from these texts is, that Christ delivered to this divinely-commissioned body of teachers a clear, definite, and precise code or body of doctrine, which they were commanded to teach just as He delivered it to them, and which they had no power to change or alter. 'Teaching them,' He said, ' to observe all things whatsoever I have commanded you.' Hence, I take it, that the doctrine and belief of the true Church of Christ must be essentially *one*. There can be no doubt as to what we must believe, just as there can be no contradiction in those doctrines which the body commissioned by Christ must teach us. The Church teaching must simply make us certain of 'all those things whatsoever' Christ delivered to it;

and as Christ could not contradict himself, neither can His Church contradict herself, which she would do if she could teach, or even sanction in any way the teaching of contradictory doctrines. Let me explain myself a little more. I will suppose that Christ commissioned the teachers in his Church to make known the necessity to salvation of baptism. If He did, it cannot be possible that He authorized another body to teach, or to sanction in any way the doctrine that baptism is *not* necessary to salvation. Christ could not contradict Himself in this way, neither can the teachers appointed by Him contradict themselves; firstly, because they are only to transmit the doctrines delivered to them; and, secondly, because He has promised to be with them (teaching) all days, to the consummation of the world. Hence, I conclude that unity of faith and belief is an essential mark of the Church of Christ. Hence, too, if I find any church teaching or allowing contradictory doctrines to be taught within her pale, I conclude that her teachings are not those of Christ. If some of her members hold the necessity of baptism, whilst others reject it as an idle myth; if some hold the divinity of our Lord, whilst others openly deny it; and so of any other doctrine; and if, whilst they are thus acting, they remain undisturbed and unrebuked in her communion: nay, more, if these contradictions arise from the very first principles which she herself lays down for them, I say, and say it boldly, that she is not of God, because God cannot contradict Himself; that it is not safe to remain in communion with her, because Christ has said that those alone shall be saved who observe *all* things whatsoever he taught; and it is evident that she teaching, or allowing her children to teach contradictory doctrines, does not observe those *all* things which are necessary to salvation. And, thirdly, if you follow me," he went on, "I draw from these texts the conviction that this teaching body cannot possibly lead one astray, or if you will have it, although I know you will make a wry face at the word—that it is infallible."

I did more than make a wry face at his words. I broke out into a loud and angry protest against them. "Well, you have reached the height of absurdity at last!" I cried. "To clothe mortal men like yourself with the attributes of the Deity! Infallibility, forsooth! But you're not serious, Eustace, you're not serious," I continued. "You're only joking. I never heard anything like it! Infallibility, forsooth!" This last exclamation seemed to me so very telling that I repeated it several times over, each time with more emphasis and effect than before.

Eustace, dear fellow, kept his temper, and took my absurdities with wonderful good humour. "When you say that I clothe mortal men with the attributes of the Deity," he rejoined, "because I assert that the Church of Christ must be infallible in her teachings, you make, my dear friend, a very gratuitous assertion, and you know, according to the old maxim, that what is thus asserted can be as lightly denied. *Quod gratis asseritur, gratis negatur.* It is one thing to say of a body of men that they are infallible by the constitution of their nature, which would be absurd; and another to say that such a body, fallible by nature, may not be infallibly protected in their teaching, so that, under certain conditions, they cannot possibly teach error. We may not be able to demonstrate with metaphysical exactitude *how* this is to be done, but if we have God's positive promise that it shall be so, this is surely enough for us. If we are to cry absurdity, forsooth, every time we cannot understand how the designs and promises of God are to be worked out, I fancy we shall have to give up a good many points of belief which we have been accustomed to hold; and if the words of Christ mean anything, so far as I can understand them, they surely bear the meaning which I, and not I alone, but all antiquity, have given them. If this body of teachers, commissioned by Christ, and sent by Him, even as He was sent by His Father, can lead us into error on matters of faith and morals, what could Christ have meant when He said, 'Behold, I am with you all days (teaching, of course, for the whole discourse was about the commission to teach) even unto the consummation of the world.' If this body can err, what did Christ mean when he said that the gates of hell should never prevail against His Church. But, above all and before all, I conclude that this body of teachers must be infallible in their teaching, because I am *bound* to listen to them, and, being bound to listen, as a necessary consequence, I am bound to *obey* them, under pain of everlasting damnation. 'Teaching them to observe all things, etc. . . . . And he that believeth and is baptized shall be saved, but he that believeth not shall be *condemned*.' Now, how can Christ, the Son of God, the eternal Justice, and the eternal Wisdom, bind me, under pain of everlasting damnation, to receive the teachings of a body who can lead me into error, who can lead me astray on matters of such momentous importance? I cannot believe anything so monstrous," he went on, his eyes seeming to flash fire, "I cannot believe anything so monstrous, and I will never believe it so long as I have the express words of Christ to the contrary. Besides, I find," he continued, "that this has always been the belief of the Primitive Church, a belief which is best proved by the fact of its practice. What else was the meaning of all those councils which met even from the earliest ages, except to declare and make known, with unerring decision, the doctrines to be held by every Christian man; and how was it that every one who presumed to hold any doctrine contrary to such decision was at once cut off as a heretic from the communion of the Church? I don't think that any man can doubt for a moment that the Primitive Church believed herself to possess this glorious gift of infallibility, and where did she get this belief if not from the apostles themselves and their immediate successors? Besides, what is the meaning of our own synods, our convocations, and our consistories, except that they are the expression of the ancient persuasion which has come down to us of the necessity of some external authority which may clear away our doubts, which may *teach* us what we are to believe, instead of sending us away to pick our own creed, as best we may, out of those inspired writings, which contain many things difficult to be understood, and which unlearned and unstable men wrest to their own destruction? This is the idea which I have formed in my blundering way, and with the help of a good deal of assistance from ———, as to the nature and constitution of the Church of Christ, and of the rule of faith by which I am to be guided and directed in my search after those things which I am bound to believe and practise. And now, old fellow," he concluded, "what have you got to say against these new and dangerous opinions of mine? Show me that I am wrong if you can. Upset my positions if you are able; only act like a thoroughly sincere and honest fellow, as you are, and don't pretend to think my views false, simply because you don't *like* them, simply because they carry us out of the beaten track, which up to this time we have been accustomed to tread."

"I shall not attempt to upset your positions, at all events not at present," I answered; "but I will merely ask you, Eustace, to tell me candidly and truly where you expect to find the realization of this ideal church which you have formed for yourself? Do you expect that these ideas of yours will be realized in the church of your baptism? because, if you do, let me tell you candidly that I think you will be grievously disappointed. The Church of England makes no claim to those wonderful gifts and prerogatives which you require in your ideal church. She seeks to impose no such yoke upon her children, but is content to allow them that share of Christian liberty which she believes her Lord intended them to have. You have laid down for yourself certain prerogatives which you contend that the Church of Christ must necessarily possess. Again I ask you do you believe that the church of your baptism either possesses or claims to possess these prerogatives and qualities? Do you believe that the church of your baptism is the Church of Christ? If you find that she neither possesses nor claims to possess those qualities which you have laid down (and I am not speaking now of the truth or falsity of your positions considered in themselves), as essential to the Church of Christ, are you prepared to give up those points and to confess that you have formed exaggerated ideas of these qualities, that you have looked for a perfection in the Church which its divine Founder never expected of it, and which, considering the elements of which it is made up, it can never have; or, on the other hand, if you cannot verify these arbitrary conditions of yours, as I consider them, are you prepared to become a renegade and an apostate from the church, to cut yourself off from her communion, to throw yourself into the arms of schism, of heresy, or of unbelief? Are you prepared to sacrifice all the glorious privileges of that Christian liberty, the possession of that simple gospel truth which you enjoy in the church of your baptism, to what I cannot but consider a mere whim, to the realization of ideas which, be sure, Eustace, are as unsound as they are arbitrary? Tell me this, Eustace, my dear, dear fellow, tell me this! I think these blunt questions of mine reduce the whole matter to its natural issue, and it is out of my deep and true love for you, out of my absorbing interest in your happiness and welfare, that I put them to you in this plain, perhaps almost rude, way. *You* will not misunderstand my motives, and, for the love you bear me, Eustace, answer these questions as plainly and as frankly as I have put them to you!

"In the first place, Ambrose," he responded, "you may be certain of one thing, that, with the help of God, I will never be a renegade or an apostate from the Church of Christ. You ask me whether, in a certain possible or impossible contingency, I am prepared to give up what you call the exaggerated ideas which I have formed as to the nature and essential qualities of the Church of Christ. I answer you with all possible candour that I am not. I have formed, after long and painful study, after deep and earnest prayer, after more struggles with myself than I care to speak about, almost than I care to remember, my idea, or, to speak more correctly, my conviction of what the Church of Christ must necessarily be. I am certain that she must be One, Holy, Catholic, and Apostolic—that there must exist in this church a supreme judge in all matters of faith, a tribunal which shall be obvious, clear, common to all, and infallible in its decisions on all matters of faith and morals. I am also sure that this supreme tribunal is not placed in the holy Scriptures alone, interpreted according to each individual's lights or fancies, any more than it is placed in the "private spirit" either of "inspiration," or of "illumination," or of "taste" or "perception,"— but that it is to be found in that divinely-commissioned and constituted body of teachers who were appointed by Christ, as I have already explained to you, and under the conditions, and with the prerogatives, which I have also explained to you. Of course, my ideas are not fully developed," he went on, "but, thus far, they are clear and explicit, and nothing will make me give them up. I may be in doubt as to where I shall, in the end, find all these ideas realized, but I have no doubt, not even the shadow of a doubt, that these ideas must be realized in the church before I will fall down in adoration at her feet, before I will confess her to be the spouse of Christ, the pillar and the ground of truth, before I will lay my weary and my aching head in trusting confidence to rest upon her motherly bosom, before I will cry aloud to her in the love and gratitude of my realized desires and ideas—'This is my resting-place for ever and ever. Here will I abide, for I have chosen it.'" He covered his face with his hands for a moment ere he went on, and, as I witnessed his earnest enthusiasm, as I listened to his ardent and reverent words, I, too, was fain to turn my head aside for a little space, that I might wipe away a tear or two, which began to trickle down my cheek. Presently, however, he resumed. "You ask me, Ambrose," he continued, "whether I look upon the church of my baptism as the Church of Christ. I will answer you as openly and as candidly as ever I can. I hope with all my heart that she is. I trust with all the sincerity of my soul that I may be able to look upon her as a true and living branch of the One, Holy, Catholic, and Apostolic Church. I trust and I pray that I may be able to find in her the marks of the true Church of Christ; that I may become certain that she is what I would fain look upon her to be, but which, I tell you candidly, Ambrose, I am by no means sure that she is. If I am to take her as the Church of Christ she must realize my idea of that Church; that idea which I have gathered from the holy Scriptures, from the Athanasian Creed, from all the teaching and all the monuments of antiquity. I am investigating her claims with all the earnestness and all the ardour of my soul, all the prayerful attention, all the study and research of which I am capable, and I confess to you, my friend, in the bitterness of my heart I confess it to you, I am perplexed and troubled beyond all measure. I am perfectly clear up to one point, viz., what the church ought to be. Beyond that, all is darkness and confusion. When I begin to strive to realize my ideas, to verify what I look upon as necessary conditions, in the church of my baptism, I am utterly bewildered and confounded. If you are not worn out and wearied beyond bearing," he went on, "I will give you just one example." I nodded my head, in token of my willingness to prolong a conversation which, to confess the honest truth, grew upon me more and more every moment, and he continued. "You know well, Ambrose, what my ideas are as to the unity which must be found in the Church of Christ. Now, as disputes and difficulties must occasionally arise, the Church of England, if she be the true church, must necessarily possess some authoritative standard of doctrine. The other day I asked my tutor, who is, as you know, considered one of the most learned men in the university, whether the Church of England really does possess any such standard. After some hesitation, which astonished me very much, he answered, yes, no doubt. Where is it to be found, I asked? After still more hesitation, he responded, Well, I suppose in the articles. Thereupon, away I went and studied the articles, together with their history, with all my might and main, and what was the upshot of it? Why, instead of coming to the conclusion that the articles are a clear and precise exposition of the doctrines which have been handed down to us from that Primitive Church, with which we *must* prove our connexion and identity if we are ever to prove that we belong to the Church of Christ, I most unwillingly came to the conclusion, that the profession of faith contained in the articles is nothing more than the merest jumble of bits of doctrine, a bit of Lutheranism, a bit of Calvinism, a bit of Zuinglism, with every here and there a bit of what is either Popery or the doctrine of the Primitive Church; and the end of it is that I quite believe what —— says, viz., that the articles were framed on no fixed principle, that they were the result of mere accident, and that they might have come down to us just as easily in any other shape as that in which we receive them; and, you know, if this be true, we might, except for that accident, have just as well been Presbyterians as Episcopalians. Another time I asked him whether the Church of Christ allowed the right of private judgment. Now, you know, Ambrose, this was a very simple question, and one which admitted of a very simple and direct answer; but I could get no definite answer from him. First he told me that we must certainly use our judgment in determining religious doctrines and belief. Then, said I, if I can use my judgment in the determination of any point of Christian belief, it necessarily follows that I can doubt about that same doctrine, and, hence, that I am at liberty to doubt, for example, about the divinity of the Son of God; but here he threw up his hands, and cried out that I should be guilty of a grievous sin if I presumed to doubt upon such a point as this. Now, what did he mean? Did he mean anything, and, if he did, did he know his own meaning? I am sure, at all events, that I could make nothing out of it, except that it was all vagueness and bewilderment, and the more I study it the more I begin to fear that really and truly the Church of England does possess no authoritative standard of doctrine at all; and that, practically, her members may believe as little or as much as they like; that it will not be safe for an earnest, sincere Christian man to remain in her communion, unless she speaks out clearly and at once to make known to us by her own voice what she is, and what she claims to be. But, oh, Ambrose," he cried suddenly, "it is a weary, weary work, and I'm almost tired to death of it. God knows I'm almost tired to death of it. May He in His infinite goodness give me light to see my way to the end of it. This is all I ask of Him—this is all I ask of Him."

"Yes, Eustace, my poor fellow," I answered, "I see that it is a weary work, and I wish that I could see the end of it. I pray God to bring you safely through it, and to remove the snares which are about your feet in His own good time; but, for the present, let us say no more on this subject." The fact was that I was very anxious to bring this conversation to a close. I did not know what to say to him. I had no solid arguments with which to meet him on those points on which he had pressed me so closely during the evening, and he was so much in earnest, he was so deeply and so thoroughly sincere, that I felt ashamed to bring forward the miserable quibbles and the stale, unmeaning arguments, or rather assertions, which rose to my lips. Hence, I concluded that the best thing I could do was to close the conversation, and take care not to renew it until such time as I felt myself better prepared to meet him. However, before we separated I took his hand once again, and spoke to him a few hurried, anxious words. "As I have already told you, Eustace," I said, "I don't profess to be very well up in these matters.

Still, I understand enough of them to see whither you are but too surely, too fatally drifting. Unless you can make up your mind to throw off by a vigorous effort these ideas which have taken such a hold upon you, I see but too plainly that you will be drawn into that false church, whose false pretensions and whose unbearable yoke our glorious forefathers so nobly cast away from them. If this should be the end of it all, Eustace, my dear friend, if this should be the end of it all, I ask you in all sober earnestness and truth, I ask you out of the depths of my heart's love for you, to tell me whether you are prepared to work out your ideas to *this* conclusion, whether you have pondered all that such a step must necessarily involve, whether you are prepared to make such a fearful plunge as that would be."

His eyes filled with tears, and for a moment or two he laid his head upon my shoulder. Presently, however, he raised his face and looked into mine with such a glance of earnest truth and love, such a glance of reverent and sincere enthusiasm, as went to my very heart, and moved me strangely in the depths of my soul. "I will do whatever God wishes of me," he said, in a low, trembling whisper, "I will do whatever God wishes of me. God is leading me, and no matter whither He leads me I will humbly do my best to follow Him. Oh, whatever else He may deny me, I humbly trust in Him that He will give me grace to follow Him whithersoever it may please Him to lead me. I trust in Him for this."

"But, Eustace," I pleaded with him, "Eustace, do you think that *God* can lead you to the Church of Rome! Oh, surely, surely, you will never let yourself be so deluded as to think that God can lead you to the Church of Rome! Surely, surely, you will never think of that——." I would have continued but my voice broke down, and I was fain to turn away my head once more that he might not see how deeply I was moved.

"Oh, don't, Ambrose, if you please; oh, don't, oh, don't," I heard him whisper in my ear, as I still kept my head turned from him. "You pain me more than I can bear to hear you talk in this wild way. I don't see any reason," he went on, "for supposing that God will lead me to the Church of Rome, but, wherever he leads me, I must surely follow. Ambrose, I must surely, surely follow!"

"Then, may the Almighty take compassion on us," I cried bitterly, "for, so far as I can see, I see nothing but troubles and tempests before us. I grieve for you, Eustace," I continued, "I grieve for you with all my heart and soul, and I grieve all the more because I am afraid that the troubles which you seem so determined to call down upon us, I say *us*, for whatever affects you must equally affect me, will have been of your own creation. I can only pray God to take compassion on you, and, most of all, to keep you clear of that which I so fearfully dread, that false faith in whose meshes I pray that your feet may not become entangled beyond all possibility of liberation. I can only pray that such a blight as this may never fall upon your young life, my friend, my friend, my poor friend."

I struggled with myself as best I could, for I was always ashamed to make any display of feeling, even before him. Spite of all my efforts, two or three great sobs rose in my throat, but I smothered them as best I was able, and turned to go away. I think I was half way down stairs on my way out when I heard him calling after me, Ambrose, Ambrose. I stopped suddenly, and waited until he came up with me. I saw at a glance that he was deadly pale, but I had only time to take one look at him before he came up to me, and laid his hands upon my shoulders, as he had a habit of doing when very much in earnest. I could scarcely catch the words he strove to speak to me they were so broken with his sobs, but I strained my ears to listen. "Oh, Ambrose, if you knew, if you only knew the load that is upon my heart, you would pity me, indeed, indeed, you would. But, no matter. Only, Ambrose," he continued, as he clung to me in his earnestness, "you will never forget the promise which you made to me this morning! Ambrose, you will never forget that!"

I could not say much to him. Many words would have been out of place. I only drew him for an instant to my breast, ere I answered in words scarcely less broken than his own. "Eustace, may God be faithful to me as I am faithful to that promise. The day will never come—my Maker, who knows my heart, sees that the day will never come—when you will have to say of me that I have forgotten my promise to you. All the world besides may cast you off, I never will. All the world besides may be unfaithful to you, but I never will. I will be faithful to you to the very end."

What was in my heart I promised him, and what I promised him I faithfully fulfilled. Through many years, not unchequered with heavy trials; through good report and through evil report; in weal and in woe; let Eustace Percy raise his voice and bear me witness whether I have kept my promise. As I write these lines his hand is on my shoulder, and it touches me as fondly and as truly as it ever did in days of yore. His breath is warm upon my cheek as he bends down to read the lines which my pen is tracing. His voice is ringing in my ears, and it is none the less sweet to me because it falters and breaks down; none the less sweet to me because it mingles with those of his wife and his innocent children; none the less sweet to me, oh surely none the less sweet, because the burthen of their cry is still the same, "Faithful evermore, faithful evermore."

END OF BOOK I.

BOOK SECOND.

IN THE DEPTHS.

"And thou, too, whosoe'er thou art,
That readest this brief psalm,
As one by one thy hopes depart,
Be resolute and calm.

Oh! fear not in a world like this,
And thou shalt know ere long,
Know how sublime a thing it is
To suffer and be strong."

CHAPTER VIII

DE PROFUNDIS.

ONCE that the ice was fairly broken between us, and now that my interest in the subject was fully awakened, Eustace and I had many such conversations as the one related in the last chapter. Although they were full of deep and absorbing interest to us, still, as I have no right to suppose that they would be equally so to my readers, and as this work most certainly does not propose to itself a controversial or doctrinal object, I shall not repeat them in this place. I will confine myself to stating, in as few words as possible, all that I must necessarily add on this subject.

Soon after the conversation recorded in the last chapter, —— went abroad, and Eustace was, consequently, left almost entirely to his own guidance in regard to those matters which, I can truly say, now absorbed every thought and energy of his heart and mind. From this period, too, I saw what I considered a very decided advance on his part towards Rome. I think he hardly realized the full bearing of his own views until, by my questions, I brought them out and developed them.

I am equally sure that he had never thought of giving names to these views, or of putting them into strict shape and form; but, when I urged him till he could not escape admitting their full bearing and significance, he never shrunk from them, because these views were clearly proved to be Roman views, and their real names Roman names; and, in this way, I brought home to him, and made him see that he was upholding and professing many doctrines and usages which were plainly Catholic, or, as I put it, Roman; and which, practically, were neither recognised nor employed by the Church of England, no matter how earnestly men, who were straining every point rather than leave the church of their baptism, endeavoured to show that, although fallen into disuse, they were, nevertheless, admitted by that church in some shape or other. Then I noticed the introduction of a crucifix, some Catholic prints, and other articles of a like nature into his room. When I attacked him about these he was always ready with his defence, and what gave me more annoyance than all the rest was, that he never defended these things on the score of their being Catholic or otherwise. He passed over that question altogether, and defended them either on the score of their antiquity, or of their reasonableness in themselves. If I rejoined that he must, however, confess that these things were not employed in the Church of England, he would only answer that he was sorry for it; and that, inasmuch as he was quite certain that they had both been employed and venerated in the early church, he was afraid that it was an additional argument to show how very far she had fallen away from many very wholesome practices and devotions. Nay, several times when I asked him whether, if the Church of England should altogether, either practically or theoretically, disown and condemn the use of these things, whilst, on the other hand, the Church of Rome nourished and encouraged their employment, he would consider this as a positive argument in favour of the Church of Rome, he answered me without hesitation, "Certainly. That church which could best prove its identity, as well in practice as in belief, with the early church, must, in his opinion, have the strongest claim to be considered the true Church of Christ." Altogether, I could not but consider him in a very bad way, and, yet, what I was to do I could not possibly see. If I attempted to argue with him he closed my mouth in a few moments. He was so thoroughly well up in his subject that I was only like a dumb dog, *non valens latrare*, before him. If I asked him to read the most rabid anti-popery or low church writings, he always willingly complied; but he read them side by side with the works of the Fathers or the productions of Catholic divines, and thus, as he said, took the poison out of them, or, as I put it, threw dust into his own eyes. And, yet, when I reproached him for acting thus, he was ever ready with his answer. "You know, Ambrose," he would say, with his gentle smile, "you know I have no object but to discover the truth, surely I must read both sides of the question;" and what could I respond to this? If I brought before him, as I sometimes did, in the strongest language at my command, the fearful rage of his father, and the utter ruin which must await him in a worldly point of view if he became a Catholic, he would shiver and turn pale, but had ever the same answer ready for me. "I am not sure that I shall ever become a Catholic, but I *am* quite sure that considerations such as those to which you allude must never be allowed to influence me either in one direction or the other; and if I am only faithful to God and my conscience, I know that He will bring me safely through every trouble or difficulty which may lie in my path." In truth, in very truth, I felt myself utterly and completely powerless to interfere between him and what I began to consider in the light of his fate. I could only look on at a distance, and, as it were, with bated breath, whilst he, for whom I would willingly have laid down my life, travelled with fearful speed along a path which I considered to be as dangerous as it was false and delusive. As I have just said, I could only bide my time and wait for the end, which I began to see clearly enough would come sooner or later. I could only prepare myself to take my part as became a faithful friend in whatever that end might bring to him; could only gird my loins and stand ready, that I might be at his side, prepared to throw the arm of my truth around him as soon as the first crash of the conflict fell upon my ears. And, in truth, although I shrank from it as from a very bitter and a very evil thing in itself; although there was scarcely a step in the world, certainly not one consistent with truth and honour, which I would not more willingly have seen him take; still, as I marked the growing paleness of his cheek, the deepening fire of his eye, the nervous restlessness of his manner, I could scarcely help wishing that whatever was to be done might be done at once; scarcely help wishing that the plunge, at once so hateful and so dreaded, had been taken ; that, so, my poor friend, if it were God's good will, might find once again the peace and rest which had been so long strangers to his weary breast. I thought that I could bear anything rather than to see him go about so worn and wan, so broken in mind and spirit, so restless in his search till he had found that which alone should be his rest for evermore, the Heart of God.

From all this you will easily conclude that I had resigned all hopes that Eustace would give give up what I had been accustomed, in my familiar way, to call " these ideas of his." I now knew well that he would never stay his steps until he had pursued these ideas to what he considered their legitimate conclusions. He had lain down for himself a notion of a church which I, from the first, had instinctively felt would never be realized in the Church of England. Not that I had ever believed his notion to be a true or a just one, but I knew that *he* considered it to be a true, nay, the only true one, and I had never been able to argue him out of it. Hence, I was like a spectator who, from a distance, watches a storm-tost sailor making his way through numberless eddies and shoals to the harbour which is before him. I stood with folded arms, so to speak, and watched him surmounting first this wave and then that, but knowing, all the while, that each wave bore him nearer to a harbour which I considered as anything but one of refuge. Still, he drifted on, on, on; ever nearer, ever in closer proximity to the dreaded shore, and still I clenched my hands and tried to nerve myself for what I felt to be before me.— Hence, too, although I was deeply and bitterly pained, I was scarcely surprised when, during one of our many conversations at this time, he told me that the whole question had begun to assume much narrower limits; that he had quite settled what the church *must* be, and that all that he had to do now was to reason out to a solution a contrariety of claims between the Anglican and the Roman Churches. I was quite as little surprised to hear him say that he had begun to fear much that the Church of England would never be able to prove to his satisfaction her claims to the four marks of the Church of Christ,—" unity" of faith and belief on all defined points—" sanctity," proclaimed by miracles and other supernatural gifts —" Catholicity," embracing all times and all ages since her foundation—" Apostolicity," derived from a regular and most clearly-defined succession of pastors from the apostles themselves. Indeed, I think he never got beyond " unity." He had always placed great stress upon this point. It was one of the first ideas which had strongly taken possession of his mind in regard to the Church of Christ, and I think he gave the Church of England up after sedulously and conscientiously studying her claims to this essential note of the church. His clear, orderly mind seemed to shrink from the disorder and confusion, the wrangling and disagreement on the most essential points, which arose, as he maintained, from the very first principles of Protestantism, but which I argued had their origin in that Christian liberty which God wishes us all to enjoy and to exercise within reasonable limits. Although his words jarred upon my ears like the notes of a choice instrument grievously out of tune, I was nowise surprised, in course of time, to hear him say that the mists were all clearing away from before his feet, to hear him openly confess that, so far as he could see, the Church of Rome could alone lay claim to be the spouse of Christ. I was, I repeat, nowise surprised to listen to his growing convictions, to his ever increasing enthusiasm. He had lain down for himself certain first principles or requirements, and these he had pursued to their legitimate conclusions. I did not admit these first principles, these primary ideas, but *if* I had admitted them, I felt that I must have drawn the same conclusion which he had drawn; and, therefore, however much I might believe him to be wrong, however deluded or deceived I might deem him, I could be no more surprised at the turn of his thoughts, than I could question the sincerity of his convictions. As I saw him drifting every day nearer and nearer to the haven before him, I could only clench my hands the more firmly, and watch him from under my knitted brows, whilst I felt that it was as useless for me to cry out to him to avoid it, as it was to pretend to be surprised when I saw him beating full into its mouth. No, the days of surprise had long since passed, and I was living in those of expectation, of anxious, wearing expectation, now. Hence, too, I was nowise surprised when he rushed into my rooms one day, and threw himself upon the ground, and hid his face upon my knees. I knew his secret well enough—I required no words to tell it to me—I saw it in his eyes—I heard it in his sobs—I felt it in his hands—I knew that the moment for which I had been preparing myself so long had come; the moment for which I had girded up my loins that I might do manfully; the moment for which I had so nerved my heart, that, forgetting myself and my own bitter thoughts, I might do my duty, my simple, honest, truthful, loving duty to my friend; and, so, without a word, I raised his face from off my knee and kissed him on the brow, as one man may kiss another, as one brother may kiss another; and this was all that passed between us when he came to tell me that the die was cast; came to tell me that he, Eustace Percy, my dearest friend upon earth, had made his election; had made a choice before the importance of which every other matter which could engage the mind or heart of a reasonable being must pale into utter insignificance; came to whisper to me, only the words failed him, that bitter news which I required no spoken words to make known to me in all its dreadful significance, in all the direful import of a meaning whose full development the future could alone unfold. This was all that passed between us on this most solemn occasion, except that, a little later on, I made him promise me to take no step, to keep his determination to enter the Catholic Church a secret for three months, and when he had heard my reasons he, with many loving, earnest words, cheerfully complied with this my strange request.

And why, think you, did I make this strange

request of him? I am almost ashamed to confess the truth. I am almost ashamed to admit that, after having proved my own utter powerlessness to arrest him in his course, to change a single one of his convictions, or turn a single one of his thoughts, on this matter into another channel, I now, in my foolish self-sufficiency, besought him to remain simply as he was, without taking another step for three months, that I, forsooth, might have time to convert him back again. This was the object, neither more nor less, which I proposed to myself. As I bent down to raise his face from my knees but a few moments before, I had vowed in my inmost heart to be true and faithful to him, no matter what might happen, and I intended to be faithful to that vow; but, at the same instant, the resolution had rushed like a flash of lightning through me to do my best, my very best, more a good deal than I had hitherto done, to win him back again from what I believed as firmly as ever to be the delusions by which he had been led away. Whether I succeeded in this or not, I would be none the less faithful to him, but I would do my best, nevertheless, to succeed in winning him back to Protestantism, or, as I more poetically expressed it, to the church of his baptism. Here was the object which I proposed to myself in begging him to take no further step towards entering the Roman communion before that day three months, an object which I did not in the least endeavour to hide from him.

And how, courteous reader, do you think I set about my purpose? What do you think I proposed to myself? It appeared to me that there was only one way of succeeding in my object, and that was by studying this system of Popery to the very bottom, so that I might be able to demonstrate its utter falsity and anti-Christian character to my friend; and to this study I applied myself with an energy which, I can truly say, I never, either before or since, devoted to the consideration of any subject. I little knew what I was undertaking, less still did I imagine what the end of it would be. In my presumption I imagined that I had only to apply the energies of my mind to this matter, and that I should surely attain my end. As I have just said, I am almost ashamed to confess the truth on this subject. I have no excuse to offer for my presumption, except my ignorance of what I was about, and my true and earnest wish to serve, as I thought, my friend. I am so certain of the purity of my motives in thus wishing to save my friend from what I deemed a great evil, that God, no doubt, gave me credit for them, and looked with an eye of pity upon my presumption. I think that he had pity, too, on my ignorance, and did not judge me so severely as I deserved, so severely as I now judge myself. I am certain that He showed me mercy far beyond my deserts, removing in His goodness, and may it be blessed for evermore, the snares from my feet, and the bandages from my eyes, at the very moment that I sat down in my pride and my presumption to do battle to my very utmost against His blessed truth, and against His holy Church. At all events, I entered at once with all my heart and soul upon the task which I had laid out for myself to do. I gave myself no rest. The early morn and the midnight hours found me toiling at my self-imposed labour. I spared myself in nothing that I might come at the truth, and, God be praised, I *did* come at the truth, although it was not what I had expected it to be. I am not going to trouble you with a long history of the course of my studies. The Catholic reader has already guessed what was, and what must necessarily have been, the result of those studies; whilst I could scarcely hope to treat of them at such length, in the space at my disposal, as would be altogether satisfactory, perhaps, or conclusive, to those of another faith. However much these latter, if, perchance, my story should fall into the hands of any such, may doubt of my powers of reasoning, however much they may question my strength of mind, however much they may pity me, let them, at least, give me credit for all sincerity. I pledge them my word, the word of a sincere, and, I trust, an honest man, that no human being could have sat down with a more prejudiced mind to the study of any subject than that which I brought to the consideration of the all-important matter on which I was engaged. The course I pursued was very simple. I allowed Eustace to furnish me with a certain number of works favouring and explaining his views and ideas. I furnished myself with those which I considered best fitted to refute those views and those ideas, and I sat down in cold blood to decide for myself between the rival claims which were before me. Of course I had not the shadow of a doubt but that my researches would end in the triumphant overthrow of Popery, and this was certainly the *primary* object which I proposed to myself, but I was also equally conscious that I was to decide between the claims of the rival churches. As I have already mentioned, I do not purpose to go into any detailed account of the workings of my mind, or of the progress of my convictions. I will tell all that is necessary in the fewest possible words. I spent at least the first month, perhaps a little more, in making up my mind as to the real idea, the nature, and the constitution of the Church of Christ. I examined and compared the different theories and views on the subject as earnestly and sincerely as a living man could do; and in the end I could come to only one conclusion. I could form only one idea, and I say no more than the barest truth when I assert that it was with a thrill of perfect horror, with a feeling of unutterable agony and dismay, that the conviction forced itself upon my mind that this idea was the very one from which Eustace had started, the very one which I had so derided and decried. For a time I *would* not believe it, I *would* not admit it. I turned away from it forcibly and sternly, as I would have turned from a fearful vision, as I would have flown from an object that was infinitely hateful and disgusting to me. I set to work and studied the whole matter over again, from beginning to end, and, yet, the result was the same. In the bitterness of my soul I was compelled to admit that the result was the same; forced to admit that if I was to be an honest man, a man who dared to act up to his honest convictions, I could blink the unwelcome conclusion no longer; and, so, in the end, although it made me groan aloud in the terror that had fallen upon my heart, I was fain to confess that there could be but one idea of the Church of Christ, that idea which Eustace Percy had so pressed upon me, that idea whose realization had led him whither I had so prayed that I might never be doomed to follow. I have spoken of the perfect horror, of the unutterable agony, of the fearful terror which fell upon me, when this thought made its way home to me, and pressed itself upon me with a persistency which I could not shake off. Yes, I was terror-stricken, for I felt that the shadow of the end was already upon me, and I shrunk from it—God knows how I shrunk from it—how utterly I loathed and detested the end that I saw before me. I had a fearful temptation to throw the whole thing up, to give myself over to indifferentism and unbelief. Again and again it came to me. Again and again the tempter whispered to me that, if I admitted this notion of the Church, I should presently be obliged to confess, as my friend had been obliged before me, that this idea could alone be realized in the Roman Church. Again and again he asked me whether I was prepared for this; and again and again I struggled, and groaned, and wept hot, scalding, bitter tears, but I went on—thanks be to God for evermore—I went on. It seemed to me as if I were drawn by a strange fascination which I could not resist. I looked upon it as a strange fascination, whilst, all the time, it was the grace of God which was moving in the depths of my unregenerate soul, only I did not know it—but still I went on. I think no man, except one who has gone through the same ordeal, can ever realize the awful character of my task from this point, until the blessed end which made all things straight. With every feeling of my nature, with every sentiment of my heart and soul, in fierce and angry rebellion against it; with all my prejudices rising up, thick and fast, to obscure my sight; with all my worldly prospects which, but a month ago, had looked so fair and flourishing, blighted and dead at my feet; worst, and most fearful trial of all, with my poor mother's sad, pale face for ever haunting me with the reproachful look, a thousand times more hard to bear than the bitterest words which human tongue has ever framed. Yes, harassed and encompassed by all these thoughts, feelings, and considerations, I still looked my subject in the face; still battled with it, for the most part, manfully and truly; still pursued my premises to their inevitable conclusions. I should have been less than a man, I think, if I could have followed out my path without now and then turning for a moment to one side; but I never threw myself back in my chair, and buried my face in an agony of grief; I never gave way for a few moments to the anguish which I couldn't master all at once, that I did not raise my head, determined, with God's help, to work my way to the end. My face grew paler, and my heart grew heavier every day, but, still I plodded along my thorny path, little heeding how my feet were torn, if, so be, I might arrive at the open country at the last. It was a fearful ordeal, God knows it was a fearful ordeal, and one to which I pray that few may be subjected. I look back at it now, and I can scarcely tell how I ever got through it, except that God was very good to me, very tender, very merciful, very considerate, far beyond my deserts. I know now, too, although I did not know it then, that he whose prayers must surely have been very acceptable to God, was on the mount with raised-up hands, praying God, morning, noon, and night, that He would have mercy on his friend; sparing his innocent flesh neither fast, nor vigil, nor scourge, that light to see and grace to do might come, in all profusion and abundance, to me. At all events, the end drew nigh, the ordeal was nearly over. I had spared myself no pains, no labour, no trouble. I had exaggerated every difficulty on the one side to the utmost. I had lowered the weight of the arguments which were against my preconceived notions as much as I had heightened those which told for me. I had left nothing undone, so far as I knew, to act like an honest and sincere man—a man who would be influenced, so far as he could help, neither by undue prejudice nor human affection. Above all things, I had endeavoured to keep my heart out of the matter. I had tried to make the whole affair one of my head and my intellect, and not of my affections or my heart; and, lo! the day was come, and I stood face to face with what I felt to be an inevitable conclusion; a necessity, a dire necessity, if you will, but still a strict, stern, inevitable necessity. As I have already said more than once, I have not proposed to show you the manner how, or the reasons by which I was led to this conclusion: I merely tell you the conclusion to which, in all honesty, in all sincerity, and in all truth, I was *compelled* to come, and it was this—that

I must, of necessity, be either an infidel or a member of the one Holy, Catholic, Apostolic Church of Rome. I question no other man's sincerity or truth. I make no reflection upon any one. I simply tell you, in the plainest words which I can use, the conclusion to which I, in the exercise of *my* sincerity, was compelled, unwillingly enough, so far as nature was concerned, to come; the conclusion to which I, as firmly as I believe that I am writing these lines in the presence of my Maker, believe that every man who studies this matter as I studied it must necessarily and infallibly come.

My mind was quite made up as to what I must do nearly a week before the end of the appointed three months. That week I spent as much as possible in solitude and prayer, and in a reconsideration of the whole matter. That I might be the less distracted, I besought even Eustace to leave me to myself until the appointed day. I had, for various reasons, kept the growth of my convictions a profound secret from him and from every one else. On the last night I scarcely went to bed, and I rose at early dawn. I struggled hard, as well as ever I could, and in prayer with God, that I might be able to overcome myself to the end, for even yet my nature and my prejudices rebelled sadly against the dictates of my intellect and will; but I never wavered; God gave me grace never to waver from what was to be done, although He did not make it the less bitter to me, perhaps that thus, in His goodness, by depriving me of sensible consolation, he might increase my merit and my reward.

Early on the morning of the appointed day Eustace came to my room. My eyes were blinded with tears, so that I could not see him quite plainly, but I saw, nevertheless, that he was very pale, and trembling with anxiety. Without a word he ran over to me and put his hands, as he had often done before, upon my shoulders. I gazed at him for a moment, as I tried in vain to form the words which stuck so painfully on my tongue. As I felt the great sobs beginning to rise in my throat, I knew instinctively that I must get it over at once, or that I should break down altogether. I made one effort to whisper it in his ear, but my head drooped down until it rested on his shoulder, as it came from me in broken, almost inarticulate, words:—

"*God help me, Eustace* (that was the way I put it), *God help me, for I must be a Catholic, too.*"

As my words fell upon his ear, he caught me to his breast and broke out into a long, loud cry. As for me, I could only sob upon his shoulder, and repeat the self-same words:—

"*God help me, Eustace, oh, God help me, for I must be a Catholic, too.*"

CHAPTER IX.

DARKENING CLOUDS.

SUPPOSE, courteous reader, some three months to have passed since the event recorded in the last chapter. They have been very eventful months to us, for, during them we have made the passage of our Rubicon, in other words, we have been duly instructed and received into the bosom of God's holy Catholic Church. Both he and I have felt to the full, have realized in our very inmost heart, that we have taken *the* great step of our lives, a step whose consequences must necessarily be of the last importance to us, must necessarily exercise an all-powerful influence and direction upon all our coming years. In the shadow of the great change that was upon us, and engaged as we have been in the absorbing duties necessary to enable us to make that change in a proper and becoming spirit, in such a way as to derive all those spiritual benefits, all those graces which ought, from the nature of things, to flow upon us on our reception into the Church, we have not as yet thought much of that future. We made our first communion on the glorious festival of

All Saints; a day to be for ever remembered by us both. From the very first God had been so good, so tender, and so merciful to poor Eustace; had filled him to such utter overflowing with His choicest consolations and His most tender gifts; had so drawn that pure, that innocent, that childlike heart to Himself, that I had looked on, as it were, from a distance, lost in wonder and astonishment at what, even yet, I could scarcely comprehend or understand. For, it had been very different with me. It pleased God to lead me by very different ways. My conversion had been one of my reason and intellect, and, up to the last, I had felt but few, scarcely any, of the consolations of God. It was only on the morning of my first communion, only when my God was reposing for the first time in my unworthy bosom, that His blessed consolations came down upon me in such abundant profusion that I was fain to bury my face between my hands, that I might hide the floods of tears which, spite of all my efforts, rained down upon the ground; that I was fain to cry aloud in the excess of my overburthened heart, Too much, O Lord, too much. I had walked so long in the stormy and dreary way of desolation that I was almost afraid there was some hidden delusion, some dangerous deceit in it, when it pleased the Lord, my Shepherd, to lead me into His pleasant and His flowery pastures, and to feed me with the waters of life; when it pleased Him to anoint my head with the oil of His gladness, and to place in my hand the chalice which inebriates with love those to whom it is given to drink; when it pleased Him to lead me into the house of the Lord that I might dwell there all the days of my life. It would be unbecoming, even if I were able, to write much on this matter. Let it suffice to say that, even if I had never received any more of God's favours, and my whole after life has been made up of them, the consolations which I received from my dear Lord's hand on the day of my first communion would more than have repaid me, aye, a thousand times over, for any little trouble or pain which I was ever called upon to bear in His sacred service. And what is true of me is true, only in a vastly higher and more exalted degree, of my friend Eustace also. Let it suffice to say that to him and to me God was good beyond all measure, beyond all degree, beyond either our deservings, which were none, or our expectations, which may have been many and great. I can only say once and for all, may His adorable name be blessed for ever and ever. *Sit nomen ejus benedictum in sæculum, et in sæculum sæculi.*

Under circumstances such as those at which I have thus merely glanced, it is nowise wonderful that we had not allowed the future to trouble us very much; but the time had now come to look it fully in the face, and the prospect was one from which stronger men than we might well have shrunk with pale faces and trembling limbs. And this was much more true of poor Eustace than myself. Of course, I knew well what a fearful blow my conversion would be to my poor mother; how it would shatter the pleasant hopes which she had cherished, and demolish the expectations which she had formed, and the castles in the air which she had built. But I had such confidence in her good sense, and still more in her love for me, as led me to believe that, when the first shock was over, she would by degrees become reconciled to what I was quite certain would, in the beginning, be a very heavy blow to her. Hence, when I wrote to her, after I had made up my mind to become a Catholic, informing her of my determination, conjuring her to believe that I had come to this determination simply and solely because I deemed it absolutely and essentially necessary for my soul's salvation, assuring her that the dearest object of all my coming life should be to minister to her comfort and her happiness, and to convince her that nothing but an unchangeable conviction of its stern necessity would ever have made me take a step which I well knew must be most painful to her, she sent me just such an answer as I expected from her. It was several days before it arrived, and when it came it was all blotted with her tears; but it contained no word of reproach, no reference to her disappointed hopes or her blighted expectations. She only told me, in a few loving words, that, as I well knew, she had no object in life but my happiness and welfare; that I was dearer to her than all the world besides; that, although she had formed hopes and cherished ideas which must now of necessity be scattered to the winds, she had as little right as she had the wish to come between me and what I felt to be my duty to my Maker. Only, she added, I must never speak to her on this matter. She would *try*, for my sake, to think as well as she could of a religion which she had always been taught to consider as very false and very wrong; but further than this she could not promise to go. She could not promise to talk to me about my great change. She could not promise to allow me to interfere, even in the most indirect manner, with her religious belief. She would *try*, nay, she *would* think me sincere, however painful it might be to her. I must act with equal forbearance towards her. She concluded by saying that we would try and love one another none the less for what was about to take place, although, she added, and here the marks of her tears were thickest on the paper, she feared, she feared very much, that we could never again be *quite* as we had been up to this.

No one can tell what a relief the receipt of this letter was to me, or how much it lessened the weight of what was before me, whilst it endeared my mother to me ten thousand times more strongly than ever. I suppose that no one but a mother, and a mother in similar circumstances, can realize what it had cost her to write it, or how every tear which had fallen from her eye upon the page had been wrung from the deepest recesses of her faithful and tender heart. There was another circumstance also which facilitated the step which I was about to take very considerably. About six months before this time a distant relation, and one from whom we had expected nothing, died, and left to my mother an annuity of some £150 a year, with reversion to me on her death. This sum, added to what she already possessed, would leave my mother in tolerably comfortable circumstances, and, of course, this left me much more free to act as I desired; since, whatever might become of me, and I had no fears about being able to provide at least respectably for myself, my dear mother was placed above the reach of want, was in nowise dependent upon me or my exertions for those little comforts which it would almost have broken my heart to see her want.

But, although God in his goodness had thus smoothed away some difficulties which had at first sight appeared very formidable to me, the affairs of my friend, Eustace Percy, wore a very different and far more threatening aspect. When I had first become acquainted with the turn which his mind was taking, I had, as you may, perhaps, remember, endeavoured to divert him from what

I instinctively saw would be the end of it all, by representing to him as forcibly as ever I was able, the grave displeasure with which it was morally certain that Sir Percy would view his son's conversion to Catholicity. Eustace had effectually closed my mouth on that, and the few other occasions when I ventured to repeat the same argument to him, by some solemn words of Holy Writ, to the effect, that every man who loves father or mother more than his Lord, is not worthy of Him; but, although silenced, I was not convinced that it would not be as I feared; nay, the more I thought of it, the more I became convinced that Sir Percy would look upon such a step as that which I knew his son would ultimately take, with the very gravest displeasure; and I saw, only too clearly, the beginning of a misunderstanding which made me tremble as I considered its probable consequences.

As soon as Eustace had finally made up his mind to become a Catholic, he had written a long and affectionate letter to his father, acquainting him with his determination, stating the reasons which had compelled him to come to this conclusion, and begging his pardon for any pain or annoyance which this step, this inevitable step, as Eustace expressed it, might cause him. Poor Eustace spent a couple of days in the composition of this letter, and he and I devoted another couple to the revision of it before, with anxious hearts, we despatched it to its destination. In the ordinary run of things, Eustace might have expected an answer on the morning of the third day after he had posted his letter. Accordingly, on that morning we looked anxiously for the post, but it brought no answer. That same evening, however, to our intense astonishment, and I may almost add, dismay, Sir Percy himself arrived, having travelled in hot haste to Oxford. He had a long and stormy interview with his son; and, although I never learnt the full particulars of it, for Eustace always strove to screen his father as much as possible, I learnt enough to know that Sir Percy had acted with the utmost harshness and severity towards his son. When it was all over, poor Eustace ran to my room, trembling in every limb, pale as death, and agitated to such an extent, that he could scarcely speak. It was a long time before I could succeed in even partially soothing him. At last, however, he became somewhat more composed; and then, from the broken sentences which escaped him, I gathered some idea of the interview which had taken place between them. "Oh, Ambrose," he gasped, as he trembled with the excess of the emotion under which he laboured, "Oh, Ambrose, it is horrible; but, *what* can I do? *What can* I do? He says that if I but dare so much as to think about this any more, he will cast me off—he will disown me—he will never again acknowledge me as child of his. He says that if I dare to disgrace him and his ancient name, by becoming a vile apostate, as he calls it, he will never forgive me—that my father's bitterest curse shall be my only inheritance. He says all these and a great many other terrible things," continued poor Eustace, trembling, until I had to support him with my arm. As he felt the pressure of the friendly hand, he drew closer to my side, and looked up to me with all the trusting confidence of the years gone by. As he placed both his hands upon one of my shoulders, and rested his face upon them, I felt instinctively that he was appealing—not in words, indeed —to my continued assistance and support. I felt that he wished to remind me, by that simple action of his, of the relations in which we had stood to one another up to this time; to remind me of that reliance which he had always placed upon me; to remind me that he relied upon me now more than ever. For my part, although at this time I had no idea of becoming a Catholic myself, I had never felt my heart so truly and so faithfully drawn to my friend; I had never felt such a simple, earnest longing in the bottom of my soul to be true to him; to let him see, now that the clouds were beginning to gather around him, that those clouds should not be without their silver lining—that the gloomy sky should not be ,without, at least, one star to point the weary wanderer on his way—to cheer his fainting heart with pleasant, though, perhaps, but distant hopes of happier and of brighter times. It was nothing to me that he was acting, as I *then* thought, foolishly. It was nothing to me that he was taking steps, and involving himself in consequences, which I *then* could not help deeming unnecessary, and, to a certain extent, rash. I say that all these considerations had no weight, no influence, not a feather's, with me. I measured my friendship, my desire to serve my friend in no such scales as these. I was old enough, and my natural character was cold and severe enough, to protect me from being carried away by undue excitement, or unjust and unworthy enthusiasm; but, on the other hand, I was young enough, and my heart and its affections were fresh enough, to enable me to put its kindly sympathies, and its generous instincts, above interest or mere worldly, calculating prudence. And by prudence I do not mean that becoming prudence, which must have its due weight in every action of rational and responsible man; but I mean that prudence, as it is called, which, no matter how a man's heart may prompt him—no matter how the generous instincts, the holy, because the true and simple sympathies of nature, which must always be the better part of his manhood, yearn and crave to have their way,—will not allow him to stir a finger to help a friend, because he cannot do so without sacrificing himself to some extent, or, perhaps, because he cannot approve of every shade of opinion, of every shadow in the actions of him whom he is called to assist. I repeat, and I am grateful for it, that, although at the time I did not think as he thought, I measured my friendship for him, my desire to be of service to him, in no such scales as these. I am thankful to be able to remember that, as he hid his face between his hands, I thought only of his needs, and not of the acts by which he had involved himself in those necessities. When, after a little while, he raised his streaming eyes, and looked into my face with such a piteous, such a wan and sorrow-stricken look as might, I think, have pierced even his father's soul, I am thankful to be able to remember how all my heart went out to him in honest manliness, in pure and simple truth. When, after a little while, he repeated the terrible threats which had fallen from his father's lips, mingling, however, with them those very different words to the effect that "he that loveth father and mother more than Me, the same is not worthy of Me," and asking me whether he could turn back, whether he could act otherwise than he was acting, I am more grateful still to remember that I answered him, "No, Eustace, never turn back so long as you are sure that God is leading you. Never be a traitor to your conscience or to truth. Whatever it may cost you, be the same pure, honest, true man that I have ever known you; and, rely upon it, my dear fellow, dearer to me than ever you were before, because you never before needed a true friend so much, that the Almighty hand which has care of the sparrow on the house top, the Almighty hand, without whose careful providence not a hair of our heads falls to the ground, will not leave you without your comfort and your support; without, sooner or later, your reward and your recompense, *magna nimis*, exceeding great." I am very thankful to be able to remember all these things—much more thankful, you may be sure, with the knowledge which I now possess, with the light which it pleased God to give me within so short a time of the incident which I have narrated in this chapter. It would have been a terrible thing if I had endeavoured, even by the slightest word of mine, to have turned away the mind and heart of my friend from the pursuit of God's blessed truth; and I thank God very humbly that He preserved me from so great an evil.

You will have gathered from this somewhat disconnected chapter that if we have not troubled ourselves much during the last three months with the future, it has not been because that future had not very strong and very urgent claims upon us. Those claims, strong as they were, have been put aside to make room for others stronger still. These latter ones, having had their full share of attention, have, in like manner, given place in turn, so far as the paramount claims of religion can ever give place to anything else; and, having endeavoured in all simplicity to discharge our duty to God, without allowing a thought of the world, or of mere worldly interest and affection to come between us and that duty; strong in our conviction that we have taken the only path that was open to us as true and honest men, stronger still in the warmth and the fervent zeal of our new-found faith, Eustace Percy and I now stand face to face, and front to front, with the future which is before us; a future which, God knows, looks gloomy enough for both of us, but ten thousand times gloomiest for him who is the least able to bear the bitter shocks, the ruthless blows which, so far as human eye can see, it most surely has in store for him.

CHAPTER X.

A MOTHER'S LOVE—FAITHFUL EVERMORE.

We have disposed of our trifling effects, taken leave of our Oxford friends, and are just on the point of starting once again for Percymoate. Several considerations have induced us to come to this determination. So far as I am concerned, I feel it absolutely necessary to retire for some little space from the hurry and the bustle of the world, that I may have time to think of the future, which must now be looked at once and boldly in the face, that I may have time to turn my attention to the plans which must now be contemplated and matured in all sober earnestness and reality; and where can I do this so well, or with so much freedom as under my mother's humble, but peaceful and secluded roof? Moreover, I have not seen my mother since my great change; and I feel that my duty, as well as my inclination, must of necessity lead me to her feet, that once again she may lay her hand upon my head—that once again her lips may press my brow, ere I go forth to take my part in the battle of life—a part which must now be so different from that which I had once expected to play. Eustace accompanies me, partly because he has nowhere else to go; but, principally, because I could not consent, under present circumstances, to allow him to be separated from me. His prospects, poor fellow, could not well wear a more discouraging aspect; and, although I strive to hope for the best, I am obliged, in the bitterness of my heart, to admit, that I see no likelihood of any change for the better.

When he had once determined to enter the Catholic Church, Eustace wrote to Sir Percy, informing him of the fact, and again imploring his pardon and forgiveness for the pain which this step might cause him. This letter was returned, accompanied by a short note from Sir Percy's man of business, to the effect, that his master declined to hold any further communication with the writer of the note, which was therewith returned. In a postscript, it was added, that any other communication from the same source, would also be returned unopened. This was no more than I had expected from my previous knowledge of Sir Percy, and, consequently, I was in nowise surprised when he took this line of conduct; but it was a fearful blow to my poor friend Eustace. It left the mark of years on him in a few days. It seemed to drive out of him, at all events for the time, that poetry which is a necessary ingredient in every high and noble nature such as his, and to leave nothing but the stern and cold realities of life, in place of the depth, the warmth, the fervid stirrings of the soul, whose every emotion is one of music, of poetry, of devotion, and of truth. I wonder whether there is anything more painful in life than to see a bright eye grow dim; to watch a fair, young cheek, grow pale; to mark a step, which, erst, was all alive with youthful energy, whose every movement was the poetry of motion in the fullest sense, all at once lose its vigour and its grace; to note the rich hair become dishevelled and uncared for, the neat dress untended and unheeded; and to know and feel that this sad change has been brought about by the blighting hand of care, which has fallen suddenly upon a heart that was as little accustomed as it was fitted to receive the rude and the heavy shock. Such was the change which had fallen all at once on poor Eustace Percy, and it was a change which was very bitter to me to witness. I never saw a smile on his face now, except when I sometimes came upon him unawares, and found him on his knees, his head thrown back, and his eyes fixed on the altar before which he was praying. Then, indeed, often and often in moments such as these, I was fain to stop with wondering steps that I might gaze for one instant ere I softly withdrew without disturbing him, upon the smile that was playing upon his face: a smile which, although I have sometimes since seen it on the countenance of those who are favoured above their fellows by God, I had never seen then; a smile which, if I may dare to say it, seems to be the reflection of the soul which, innocent of hand and clean of heart, pierces even in its mortal flesh to the very presence of its God. But, when he had turned away with a sigh from the foot of the altar, the shadow passed across his face, the weight fell upon his heart, and I scarcely knew him for the Eustace Percy of a few short months ago. And it was not because there must be a change in his circumstances, because, in all probability, he must take a position somewhat, perhaps a great deal, lower in the social scale than the one which he had held up to this time. These considerations would have caused him but very little trouble. But it was the thought that the love of long years could be so lightly cast away, that he could be so cruelly and so harshly punished for following the dictates of his conscience, which weighed so heavily upon him, and pressed him to the very earth; which carried him beyond all my efforts to comfort and console him. As it was, I could only leave him to God, hoping that He would, in His own good time, bring about a happier and more cheering state of things, at the same time, however, resolving that, for the present, I would not allow poor Eustace to separate himself from me. When I invited him to accompany me to my mother's little cottage at Percymoate, he accepted my invitation at once, and with many expressions of gratitude. In doing so he had motives which, at the time, I never suspected, and which, if I had suspected them, would most certainly have deterred me from allowing him to accompany me to Percymoate. I would have requested my mother to meet us in some other locality. I acted as I deemed the best, under the circumstances, and my ignorance must be my excuse for my share in the unfortunate and unforeseen events which followed.

We travelled down to Percymoate on the old stage coach, and for the first time in my life, I did not find my mother waiting for me on our arrival. I guessed, however, that she was afraid to meet me in public; and so, begging Eustace to remain a little while at the hotel, where we had alighted, I hurried away to my mother's cottage. My heart beat very fast as I entered the gate of the garden which led up to the door. Another moment, and nerving myself for what I feared might be a very painful scene, I threw open the door, and rushed hurriedly into the parlour where my mother usually sat. She was sitting at a table; but, as I entered, she rose from her seat as if to meet me. I think she had scarcely advanced a single step ere she sat down again, and turned her face away from me. I ran over and threw myself upon my knees before her, and strove to take her hand in my own. She drew it gently, but yet, hastily away—still kept her face turned from me, and spoke not a single word to me. Such a greeting—so unlike the one I had ever received in the days gone by, was ineffably painful to me. Of course, I was thinking only of myself, and not of my mother. I made no allowance for all she must feel on such an occasion as this; no allowance for her buried hopes—for the expectations which were once so bright and fair; and which, so far as she was concerned, were now lying in a withered heap at her feet. I thought only of myself—of the affection of former years—of meetings which had been so full of love and bliss; and so unlike— oh, so unlike, to this. Her seeming coldness appeared to me so unreasonable, and so unkind, that it stung me to the heart. I thought that she, at least, might have made some allowance for me. I thought that she, at least, might have understood how much the step which I had taken had cost me; that she, at least, might have appreciated my motives, might have given to my weary heart, at least, the solace and the comfort of a motherly welcome. In the hasty petulance which had so grievously misunderstood her I was about to rise from my knees; but, a moment more, and I felt her hands entwining themselves fondly in my hair, as they had so often done when I had knelt, an innocent and loving child, at her feet. A moment more, and a shower of burning tears was raining down my neck and face. As I raised my head to look her in the face, that face came drooping down to mine with all her mother's love, her mother's heart, her mother's instinct for her only child burning in the eyes which met my own with such a fond, a longing, and impassioned gaze. A moment more, and her arms were tight about my neck, her head was resting on my breast, her tears were falling to my feet. And, then, she sobbed and cried, "My child, my child. I had not thought of this, and God only knows how hard it is to bear; but, still, my child—oh, surely still, my darling, darling child." I knew that all her mother's heart had rushed out from her in those simple words; and, as I drew her to me, as I held her in my arms, as I mingled my tears with her own, I strove to tell her all that I would fain have said to her, strove to tell her how I had vowed to God to love, and tend, and cherish her through all the coming years more tenderly than I had ever done; only my tongue refused to speak, my lips refused to form the words, and all that I could do was to strain her more and more fondly still to my breast; all that I could do was to utter ever and anon the simple word which spoke in all its eloquence to her mother's heart, the simple word which had been the first my infant lips had formed, the simple word which so many a time I had breathed upon her breast, but which I had never uttered with a tenderer love, with a more childlike simplicity, with a deeper and a truer devotion than I did now, as I bent down my face to hers, and whispered in her ear, and called her, in all the fulness of my burning love, by the holy name of *Mother*.

After the first passionate burst of love and pain was over, my mother exerted herself nobly to make me feel at my ease. As I have already said, there was a tacit understanding between us that I was not to speak to her on the subject of religion, and this understanding I had no desire, at all events, for the present, of breaking through. As soon as we were sufficiently composed I returned to the hotel for Eustace, and if anything could have given me a higher idea of my mother, or have endeared her more to me, it would have been her reception, at once so motherly, so considerate, and so gentle, of poor Eustace; and I had not seen him look so happy for some time as he did that evening, as we three sat far into the night, chatting pleasantly and simply together.

It was late when I led Eustace up to the little room which had been prepared for his reception. I had shaken hands with him, and after a few kind words, was about to leave him for the night, when he suddenly stopped me. "If it be not too late, Ambrose," he said, "let me have one word with you. I have something which I am very anxious to say to you at once."

I immediately closed the door, and sat down by his side, somewhat anxious, I confess, to hear what he had to say to me.

He did not attempt to speak for a few seconds, but sat with his face buried between his hands. I was just about to recall him to himself by some little action or other, when he raised his face, and turned it towards me. I remarked a hardness about his mouth, and a look of determination upon his countenance, which I had never seen there before, and which somewhat surprised me at the moment. His brow darkened, and his mouth began to twitch, but there was no mistaking the meaning of the words which came from him, as if with a sudden jerk: "Ambrose, I *must* see my father."

It had never entered into my mind that he would contemplate such a step as this; one, from which, under the circumstances, I could anticipate nothing but trouble and misfortune. It took me so much by surprise, and it also alarmed me so deeply, that it was a moment or two before I could answer him.

"I trust, Eustace," I said, at last, "that at present you will do no such thing. You ought to know Sir Percy better than I do; but I think that I know him well enough to be able to see that such a step on your part would be very imprudent, and could have no good result. Pardon me, if I speak plainly, but you know your father's proud, unbending disposition. You know how bitterly, and, just at present, how fiercely he resents the step you have taken; how he thinks that you have slighted his authority, disregarded his feelings, and brought disgrace upon his name. Of course, he is very wrong, and very unreasonable in all this; but, my dear friend, we must

take him as he is, and not as he ought to be.
When we consider how we may best bring him
round to better and more generous feelings, we
must consider him in the concrete, with his
wounded pride, his anti-Catholic prejudice, his
spirit irritated and galled to the last degree. *We*
know the truth, and the beauty, and the holiness,
of the Catholic religion. *He* does not; and we
cannot, therefore, expect him to act as if he did;
and we must make all due, and, if necessary, a
great deal of undue allowance for him. You know
well, dear Eustace—surely you know well that I
would be the last to counsel you to any act which
might seem wanting, either in duty or respect, to
your father. You know well what a great and a
blessed privilege I would deem it, to be able to
lead you to your father's feet—to cause the kiss of
peace and reconciliation to pass between you two.
You know, and you feel all this, Eustace," I continued, " but I am quite convinced that the reconciliation which you so ardently desire, but not less
ardently than I do, will not be furthered, but, on
the contrary, will be retarded; that the feelings
of irritation under which he labours, will be fos-
tered—that his anger and his pride, all unreasonable as it is, will be increased a thousand-fold, by
endeavouring to force yourself upon him at present. No: give him a little time to reflect on
all these things. He is a man of high and noble
qualities; and when time, the great soother of all

sorrows, has blunted the first sharp edge of his pain, depend upon it, he will begin to see the unreasonableness of his conduct. Without I mistake him, grievously," I went on, and, alas! I did mistake him to a great degree, "to see the unreasonableness of his conduct is, with him, to repent of and change it. Give him a little time, and the instincts of his father's heart, must surely begin to make themselves felt within his breast. Give him a little time, and that heart must surely begin to yearn to his child. No matter how a child may offend—no matter how he may go astray, and, strictly speaking, you have neither offended nor gone astray—the parent's heart must re-assert its rights in the end; holy nature must surely make herself felt and acknowledged. Remain, then, quietly for a little time with us. My mother shall be your mother, and my mother's son shall be your brother; but, Eustace, dear, dear Eustace, do not be rash. Do not by rashness and precipitation, complicate an affair which is already unfortunate enough. Remember, too," I added, as the recollection of my Lady Percy, the stepmother of Eustace, flashed vividly across my brain, "remember, too, Eustace, how much need you have to act with caution; and, for God's sake, promise me," I added, very earnestly, "promise me that you will not attempt to see your father at present. That would ruin all."

I had kept my eyes fixed upon him as I spoke

thus to him in hot and hurried words. I was pained beyond measure to see that his mouth never relaxed, that his brow grew none the less dark, that the look of determination only settled more deeply on his face. He passed his hand wearily once or twice across his brow, but when at length he spoke, it was only to repeat the self-same words in a more determined tone than ever. "It is no use, Ambrose, it is all no use, I *must* see my father. I shall never be happy, my heart will break, if I do not obtain his forgiveness. If I can only speak to him just for one moment, if I can only get just one opportunity of explaining to him how all this has come to pass; when he understands, as I am sure I can make him understand, that I have only acted as I have done because I felt that the salvation of my soul was at stake, he will relent, and take compassion on my misery. You know, Ambrose," he went on, "how deeply and how truly I have ever loved and honoured him; and if a shadow ever came between us I never loved *him* the less for it, because I never attributed it to him. You know that I have never contradicted him, never thwarted him, never gone against his will except in this matter; and he must understand, oh, surely, he must understand that, in this matter, I was not free, that I could not help myself; and he cannot be angry with me, he cannot disown me and cast me off for following the dictates of my conscience. I am afraid," he continued, and his brow grew darker as he spoke, "that some one is poisoning his mind against me. I am afraid that I have an enemy somewhere who, for his own ends, is hardening my father's heart against me; and I have no way of meeting this, I have no chance of reinstating myself in his favour unless I can gain access to him. No, Ambrose," he added excitedly, and with such stern determination as made me begin to fear that I should never move him from his purpose, "No, Ambrose, I *must* and I *will* see my father at any cost. I am not the less sensible of your kindness, and I thank you for it from the bottom of my soul, but I came down here simply and solely that I might see my father. Nothing will move me from this determination. I have no consequences to fear. I do not seek for his wealth. He may divide every shilling which he has between Rupert and his little child, and I will not repine, I will not question his right to do so. I seek nothing but his forgiveness, nothing but his love; but, if my heart is to be broken, it may as well be broken at once. If I have nothing to hope for, I may as well know the worst at once, and, at all events," he cried, rising hastily from his chair, as if he thus signified to me his final and irrevocable determination, "at all events, I *must* and I *will* see my father."

Ordinarily speaking, my friend, Eustace Percy, was one of the most gentle and the most tractable of human beings. Under ordinary circumstances my influence over him was almost unlimited, but at present I was utterly and completely at fault. I have often remarked that men such as he, when once they have come to a fixed conclusion on any point which is marked out to them by religion, duty, or strong affection, are as immovable and as firm in their determination as, under ordinary circumstances, they are gentle, easily moulded to other men's opinions, and distrustful of their own. I argued the matter with him earnestly, for a long time, and under every point of view; but, whilst he was ever loving and affectionate in his words to me, whilst he exaggerated every little service which I had ever done him, whilst he spoke of me and what he called my faithful friendship in terms which I cannot repeat, the end was ever the same, the unvarying determination expressed in the words which seemed to come from out his very heart, "It is no use, Ambrose, it is all no use, I *must* and I *will* see my father." And so at last, out of very pity to his poor, pale face; out of very pity to his tears, his sobs, and his weary cry; out of the very pity which made me prize and revere him more and more deeply every moment of his life, I gave up the useless contest. I urged my opposition no farther, although I felt none the less surely, none the less keenly, that my poor friend was but about to draw the storm more fiercely down upon his unprotected head, to entangle his bleeding feet but still more deeply among the cruel thorns which had so suddenly sprung up around his path. I had but one comfort and one consolation in all this. It came to me more strongly than I had ever before felt it, as I was that night pondering in the silence of my own room on the present and the future of my friend. It was the holy and the blessed thought that, however dark the path of life may grow —however apparently inextricable the confusion may become—however the winds may howl and the waves may roar—however little we may be able to see that end, there is One, nevertheless, who is ever causing all the troubles and the pains of this weary life to work together for the good of those who follow Him with simple and with loving hearts—One who is ever tempering the wind to the shorn lamb—One who has sworn not to break the bruised reed nor quench the smoking flax—One who has told us in words that shall never fail, for they are the words of truth itself, that happy is the man who suffereth pain, and trouble, and temptation—who has told us that they who go forth sowing their seed in weeping and in tears shall surely return in great rejoicing, carrying the sheaves of the harvest time which shall compensate, even to the very full, for all the former things that have passed away.

CHAPTER XI.

THE BURSTING OF THE STORM.

Before I retired to rest that night, I had made one resolution, viz., that if I could not prevent my friend from endeavouring to see his father, I would, at least, wait upon Sir Percy previously, that I might thus judge as much as possible, for myself, of the real state of affairs, and if I had an opportunity, pave the way for Eustace. Probably, I acted indiscreetly enough in this; but I can only say that I did all for the best; and this must be my excuse. Moreover, in any case I should have waited upon Sir Percy. He had been so kind to me, and his intentions in my behalf had been so generous, that I deemed it no less than my duty to wait upon and personally inform him of that change in my position of which he had, doubtless, already heard from other sources. Consequently, the very next morning, after making some excuse to my mother and Eustace for my absence, I made my way with no little trepidation of heart to Percy Grange. I doubt whether I had ever, even in my youngest days, entered it with more nervousness and trembling than I did on the present occasion. However,

I called all my resolution, all the strength of my manhood to my aid, and boldly sent up my name.

After some delay the servant returned, and begged me to follow him to Sir Percy's room. How my heart did beat, to be sure, as I trod the noble galleries and the stately halls of the grand old house—the house from which one certainly, if not two, of its sons were exiles and outcasts. Raising a thick curtain of heavy velvet, the servant threw open the door, and once again I stood in the dreaded presence of Sir Percy Percy. As I entered by one door, I caught a glimpse of the skirts of my Lady's dress, as she vanished through an opposite one, and I instinctively felt that her presence at such a time, boded me no good. As if to provide against any danger of her influence suffering by her absence, she had left her son behind her. He was now a very handsome child of some four years of age. He was standing by his father's knee as I entered the room; and he at once reminded me most forcibly of what Rupert and Eustace, the two elder sons of Sir Percy, had been when I first knew them. However, I gave no more than a passing glance at him, for, as I need scarcely say, my whole attention was at once directed to Sir Percy.

A little more frigid in his manner, perhaps—the expression of his mouth a little more cold and cynical—his face a little paler, and more careworn than usual—he was, with these trifling differences, which an ordinary observer would scarcely have noticed, the Sir Percy I had always known, as he rose from his chair, as I entered the room, and received me—if with coldness—with all the dignity and politeness of a gentleman. As I stood hesitatingly on the threshold, feeling all the awkwardness of my position, and scarcely knowing how to act, he advanced a step towards me, and held out his hand. Although there was no warmth, no feeling in its grasp as it touched mine, he gave me his *hand* nevertheless. Sir Percy was far too much of a gentleman to have offered me *a couple of fingers*—a detestable practice which is in vogue with some who do not think you good enough to give you a whole hand; and who, being obliged to notice your presence, do not like to be rude enough to refuse you the ordinary salutation which one Englishman pays to another, and so make a compromise between your nothingness and their gentility, by extending to you a couple of their fingers—a piece of condescension which I am always grievously tempted to acknowledge by taking hold of the said fingers, whenever they are extended to me, with the lap of my coat. He motioned to me to take a seat; inquired politely after my own health, and that of my mother; and, having gone through these conventional formalities, waited with frigid politeness for what was to follow.

I had scarcely ever felt less at ease; but, at last,

I made a dash at it, and plunged at once, *in medias res*, to the heart of the business which had brought me into his presence. " You have always been so kind to me, Sir Percy," I began in a hesitating and blundering way, " and your intentions in my regard were so generous, so truly liberal, that I have deemed it my duty to wait upon you, in order that I might personally inform you of a very considerable change which has lately taken place in my position, and of which, perhaps, you may have already heard. I have not the presumption to suppose that my future lot can be of any interest to you," I ventured to add; " but still, Sir Percy, I hope you will do me the justice of believing that I have not taken so grave a step without the weightiest reasons; and if, by any chance, I can have offended or given any pain to you by that step, I trust that you will pardon me for it, and believe that it was as unintentional as it was unforeseen by me."

Sir Percy listened to my speech with the attention which politeness demanded of him, but without showing any interest in it. The slightly-raised eye-brows might, and possibly did, express some little astonishment, that I thought it worth my while to trouble him with these remarks; but beyond this, not a muscle of his face moved. I could not tell, at the moment, whether he really felt so utterly cold and indifferent to me as he pretended to do, or whether he were merely playing a part; but I felt that if he were playing a part, he was, at all events, playing it to perfection.

When he answered me, it was in words, the tones of which were cold and cutting to the last degree. "As the son of one of my earliest friends," he began, "I need not tell you, that you must always be welcome to my house; but you have made a great mistake in supposing that you were under any obligation of coming hither to inform me of the step which you have lately taken—a step, of which, of course, I have heard, and which, I need scarcely tell you, I regret very much, both for your own sake, and that of your poor mother. It is quite true, that I have taken an interest in you, but not greater," he went on with lofty coldness, "than it was fitting for me to take in the son of a man whom I once loved and esteemed. It would be out of the way if I were to attempt to deny that I proposed to myself to serve you, and promote your interests in so far as I might be able, because I have already made my intentions known to you. You, in the exercise of that discretion which I must suppose you to possess," he went on, his words cutting like razors, "have thought fit to take a step which necessarily frustrates my intentions, whatever they may have been in your regard, which deprives me of any power, and I will be very frank with you, and add, of any great desire to interest myself in your future career. I may regret all this; but, after all, it is your affair and not mine. Young men will be young men, and act foolishly to the end of the chapter; but, so long as they do not cause others to feel the effects of their foolishness, I do not see that we need distress ourselves very much about it. I am quite sure that *you* have acted very foolishly; and, now that you have introduced the matter, although quite unnecessarily, I will add, that I am sorry for it;—sorry for your mother's sake, sorry for the sake of your father's memory, and sorry, even for your own sake; but, having said thus much, I will only repeat that you made a great mistake in supposing that you were under any obligation whatever of mentioning this very unpleasant matter to me. I assure you that it can possess no interest whatever for me."

I had expected that he would take this matter very coolly, but I had not anticipated that he would take it so coolly as this. My hot blood rushed indignantly to my face with a feeling of shame and confusion that I had so humbled myself as to speak of a matter, which was so near and so dear to me, to one who not only felt no interest in it, but did not even take the pains to conceal that want of interest. I was about to make some further remark to the effect that I was sorry that I had thus troubled him, but, before I could utter the words, he laid his hand upon my arm. " Excuse me, my young friend," he said, more coldly than ever; " excuse me, but I think we had better say no more on this matter. It cannot be very pleasant to you, and to me it is unpleasant in the last degree, and I must decline to hold any further conversation on the subject."

He said these last words in a tone which admitted of no reply, and I rose to my feet. Up to this point, although cold as ice, he had been perfectly polite, and, whilst I felt indignant with him in my heart, I could scarcely find a reason to myself why I should be so. I was to probe him now on a tenderer point. He put out his hand to me as I rose to depart, and whilst I held it in my own I determined, at every risk, to make one effort on behalf of my friend. "Pardon me, dear Sir Percy," I said as warmly, but as respectfully as ever I could, "if I venture to say one word more to you on behalf of one whose interest is as dear to me as my own, nay, I think, dearer. As you are doubtless aware, your son Eustace has become a Catholic too——."

I had touched him to the quick at last, and, spite of all his coldness, all his pride and haughty reserve, he winced beneath the touch. He let my hand fall as suddenly as if it had stung him. His face grew deadly pale, and a light, that made me tremble as I saw it, gleamed in his eyes. The Percy face is glorious in its manly beauty, but it is one which I would fain be preserved from beholding when the image which its Maker impressed upon it has been driven away, to make room for the expression of those hidden passions which so distort and blacken the fair work of the Creator's hand. An instant, a second, and that terrible expression had gone, but it made an impression upon me which I have never forgotten. As he recovered himself he sat down again on the chair from which he had just arisen, and drew to his side the innocent child who was gazing at him with wondering eyes. Strange contradiction! He put away the golden curls which should have reminded him so strongly of that other child who was yearning with all the longing of a sickened heart, of a heart weary with hope deferred, yearning for the words of peace and forgiveness, which alone he 'asked at his father's hands, and with which, as his only fortune, the only wealth he sought, he was content to face the world. Yes, he put away the golden curls from his child's fair face that he might kiss him on the brow ere he uttered the cruel words which should have blistered his false tongue ere they had come forth to be written down against him by the recording angel's faithful hand—the cruel words which his false pride, his unreflecting bigotry, his unreasoning anger, and wounded self-love drew forth from his father's heart—aye, even from his father's heart, save the mark—to cast a deadly blight upon the budding hopes, upon the young life so full of promise and expectation, of as true, as faithful, and as noble-souled a son as ever walked the world. Without one faltering tone in his voice to tell of the conflict which must have been raging in his heart, without one quiver of his proud lip, without the vestige of one tear in his cold, stern eye, as smoothly and as glibly as if the foul words were but the whispered benison of a father on his fondest child, he looked me full in the face as he uttered the sentence which, for the sake of our common manhood, I am almost ashamed to write upon this page.

"I beg your pardon, sir," he said, "but you make a great mistake. No son of mine has been guilty of such an absurdity as that to which you allude."

Not a syllable more! As his words fell upon my ear I was conscious that all my angry blood rushed up into my face. I felt the very ends of my fingers tingling with indignation and anger. I felt as if my whole soul were gleaming in indignant protest out of my eyes; but, before I could find vent for the bitter words which were trembling on my tongue, he took me up again, and went on as coldly and as sternly as before. "My eldest son, Rupert, is, as perhaps you are aware, upon the continent. I have no reason to suppose that he has disgraced either himself or me in the manner to which you refer. My youngest son is before you. I need scarcely add that he is too young to have disgraced me either,—and—and—" he faltered for one brief moment ere he added, "and—*I have no other child. I have no other son save these two.*"

Not a quiver on his lip when, after that momentary pause, he uttered these false and cruel words. As he saw that I would speak now in spite of him, he rose from his chair, as if to prevent me, and laid his hand upon my arm. I threw it off with a feeling of disgust, which I did not take the trouble to conceal. " You have no other child," I cried aloud in irrepressible indignation. " You have no other child but these two! May God forgive you, Sir Percy Percy, your false, your cruel, your unnatural words! Nay, sir, you *shall* hear me," I went on, as he raised his hand as if he would strike me in the torrent of rage which I could see sweeping, as it were, over his whole being at my hot and angry words. " If you never hear the truth again you shall hear it once at least. You have no child save these two! You have, and you know it well. Let your proud heart speak the truth, and it will tell you that you have as pure, as noble, and true-hearted a gentleman for your son in Eustace Percy as ever blessed a father's love. How true to you in every thought —how lavish in his love—how humbly obedient in his every act, save where the salvation of his soul came into collision with what you falsely suppose to be his duty to you—how jealous of your honour, and how proud of you and your fair fame he has ever been—all this and a thousand times more you know full well. You know that Eustace Percy never wronged you by his slightest thought. You know, or you might know, that it has nearly broken his heart to go against your will even in this matter, where you have no more right to interfere between him and his Maker than I have right to interfere between you and the God who will, I trust, forgive you the fearful words which it has been my evil lot to listen to from your lips to-day. Nay, sir, hear me to the end," I continued, as, in his bitter indignation, he again raised his hand with a threatening gesture. " I speak not for myself, and I fear you no more than I fear the poor child at your feet. I speak in the cause of innocence, and of truth, and of justice, and you shall hear me out, for, on this matter, you need not fear that I will ever again humble myself to address a word to you. I repeat that you might have known how much this step has cost your son, and if you did but know one half of what he has suffered, if you did but know one tittle of the crushing weight of sorrow and of bitterest pain which has fallen on his life's young spring, instead of hardening your heart against him who has committed no crime against you, except that of following the dictates of his conscience, you would surely relent—the pleadings of nature would surely make themselves heard within your breast—you would surely take compassion on your own child, the child who is crushed to the very earth by the load of sorrow and of pain which has been laid upon him, even by his father's hand——."

"And do you think, sir," he cried, interrupting me, furiously, as that evil expression crept across his face once more, marring all its beauty and its stately comeliness, "and do you think that *I* have nothing to bear? Do you think that *I* have had nothing to suffer? Do you think that it is nothing to me—to me who can point back through a long line of ancestors, and dare any man to say that one of that line ever brought shame upon the noble name he bore—do you think that it is a matter of no consequence to me that a boy who bears my name, who has my pure blood within his veins, who has sat at my table, and had a place, with shame I say it, had a place in my hopes, can so far forget himself, so far forget what is due to me, and, if not to himself, at least to the hitherto untainted name which he bears, as to commit an act which makes my blood boil with indignation, which makes me tingle with shame, as I do but think of it? How dare you, young man," he cried with a terrible voice, which made me begin to tremble before the storm which I had stirred up, "how dare you prate to me of honour, and of purity, and of truth? What regard had he for *my* honour when he cast it to the winds, when he made me a laughing-stock and a byword to my fellows? Why, I am ashamed to show my face,

I am ashamed to go abroad. For the first time in my life, I am ashamed to look even my own servants in the face. Do you think that it is nothing to me to be pitied by my own menials? Is it nothing to me to have the hateful finger of scorn pointed at me as a man who could not rule his own family, as a man who allowed his own son to become an apostate, a renegade from the faith of his fathers, from the faith for which some of his ancestors bled and died? (Poor man, in his blindness, he forgot that more of his ancestors bled and died for that faith to which his son had but returned.) Do you think that it is nothing to me to be obliged to listen to the still more hateful words of condolence which men presume to pour upon me till my whole soul grows mad with rage? Tell me, I say," he went on, more excitedly than ever, " tell me, you, who are so eloquent, you who can prate so fluently about honour and truth, do you think all this is nothing to me? And who is he, a mere beardless boy, that he dares to place his whims, his boyish fancies, for they are no more, in comparison with *my* honour, with my unsullied name, with my truth, which never knew a blot till the evil day when a Percy was found to disgrace the escutcheon of his family? Do you think it is nothing to me that I have nourished a viper which has crept out upon me and stung me to the quick, inflicted upon me a deadly wound, which neither you nor any such as you can ever realize? Silence, sir," he cried, as I was about to reply in terms as fierce as his own to the insult which he thus cast upon me: " Silence, sir. I allowed you to have your say. I allowed you to plead the cause of a traitor, and, although I demean myself by it, I will have my say now. I tell you, that he who has acted thus, is no son of mine. He may bear the Percy name—the Percy blood may purple his veins—but, he is no Percy, for all that. A Percy never yet forgot the honour or the dignity of his name. He has forgotten both—he has trampled them beneath his feet—he has done his best to make our noble name—a name so great, so glorious, till he bore it—a by-word and a scoff; and I will never forgive him for it. Men shall know, at least, that if I cannot rule my family, I can cast them off—disown them—tear the very memory of them from my soul, when it has come to that pass. And, so, I tell you, sir," he continued, in the same terrible voice—the same terrible light gleaming out of his eyes—the same terrible agitation shaking his whole frame, till he trembled like an aspen leaf; " and so, I tell you, sir, and you can bear the message to him in whom you take such an interest—he has disregarded me and all my dearest interests, and so, I disregard him: he is no more to me than the veriest beggar who walks along the street: he has chosen his own path, and he may pursue it; but, let him not dare to cross mine. If he does, I will tread him beneath my feet as I would the foulest reptile that could crawl athwart my steps. I would rather have seen him dead before my eyes. I could have stood over his open coffin—the grief with which I should have kissed the cold face of my boy, if I could only have laid him in his grave with honour—would have been luxury, compared with what I feel to know that he lives, a dishonour and a disgrace to himself and to me. As it is, I will tear the very image of him from my heart. I will strive my very best to forget the ungrateful boy, who, to my shame and reproach, bears my name. I will proclaim it to the world, as I proclaim it to you—he is no son of mine, and I will never look upon his face again!" As he uttered the fearful words, he turned his back upon me; and again, strange contradiction, drew to him the innocent child who had been listening to him all this while, with a wondering and a terrified look upon his fair, young face.

I walked over to him and laid my hand gently and respectfully upon his shoulder. Spite of all his bitter language—his fierce indignation—his unreasonable anger against his son—(his harsh words, and his insults to myself, I did not heed the moment they had passed)—I could not but pity him. It was a terrible sight to see such a noble nature so sadly warped aside; to see how ruthlessly—how recklessly, he could cast away from him, as a thing not worth the having—the generous love, the warm and pure affection of his son's true heart; to see how remorselessly he could trample all that love and all that affection beneath the feet of the idol which his pride had raised aloft upon the ruins of his shattered love. Is there anything in the world so dreadful in the fierceness of its unreflecting anger—anything which so blots out the past with all its pleasant thoughts, its innocent recollections, its sunny memories of the days gone by—anything which so hardens the heart against everything which is true, and holy, and just, as religious bigotry, when it once takes possession of a nature which is naturally haughty and proud, naturally sensitive and honourable? And how much worse it becomes when this bigotry is continually fed and kept alive by open accusation, by covert insinuation, from the lips of one who is ever at the elbow of him who is under the influence of this madness, one who has continual freedom of speech, who speaks with all the weight which love and trust ever command? Such I believed to be the case with poor Sir Percy. I saw that his pride had been touched to the very quick; that his honour, as he thought, had been slighted, and himself disgraced. I saw him labouring under the influence of many unreasonable passions—passions which were scarcely less unreasonable than they were violent, foremost amongst them, religious bigotry. I had reason to believe, or, at all events, I could not help believing, that one who should, under every point of view, have been a peace-maker was, for her own ends, whatever they might be, feeding and fomenting the flames, casting oil instead of water upon the raging fire of passion and of prejudice. I took in all this, and a great deal more which I cannot describe, in a moment; and, therefore, much as I blamed Sir Percy, bitterly as I resented his harsh conduct towards a child so worthy of far different treatment at his hands, I could not but pity him even from the very bottom of my soul. Hence, as I have just said, I laid my hand gently but respectfully upon his shoulder:

"Dear Sir Percy," I ventured to say, " in all human probability this is the last time I shall ever trouble you with my presence. You can never know how grateful I am to you for all that you have done for me, for all that you intended to do. Pardon me, if I venture to ask you as a last request to think better of this. Depend upon it, you will regret the bitter words which you have used this day. Depend upon it, the day will come when you will be only too glad to look once more upon the face of him whom you thus cast away from your heart and love."

Almost before the words had left my lips he turned upon me as angrily as ever. He rang the bell violently to summon a servant to show me to the door. "Go, sir," he cried with a hasty gesture, and in a tone which left me no alternative but to obey, "go, sir, and for God's sake leave me alone, for I can bear no more of this."

Without another word, without the formality of a leave-taking, which, under the circumstances, would have been a mockery too bitter to be enacted by men who were so terribly in earnest as we were, I turned away and left him there, his hand pointing imperiously to the door, the fearful look glaring out more hideously than ever from his face, his little child clinging in terror to his knees. Such was my last sight of him, and it was one never, never to be forgotten.

As I was passing through the hall to leave the house which already possessed so many painful recollections for me, I came suddenly upon my Lady. She was standing motionless as a statue, at some little distance from the door by which I must necessarily pass out. She made no attempt to approach to me. She vouchsafed me never a passing word. She cast upon me one haughty glance, and I thought I had never seen her look half so handsome as she did standing there, with such an air of pride, of exultation, and of triumph, on her beautiful face. But though she spoke to me not a single word—though she cast upon me but one haughty glance as I passed her by—I knew instinctively that she was a wicked woman. I had always thought, I had always feared it, but I knew it now, knew it better than if I had seen it written on her brow in letters of living fire—

knew that she was a proud, scheming, ambitious woman—a woman who had shrunk from no misrepresentation, from no open slander, no covert insinuation, that she might harden the heart of the father against his child, that she might gain the triumph for herself which I saw glancing out of her eyes, and gleaming in every feature of her face, as her evil look fell on me whilst I passed as quickly as I was able from her presence.

And for him, that poor, unhappy, miserable, deluded father! Had he been in sad, sober earnest all this while, or had he been but acting a base and wretched part? If he had been but acting a part, it was but sorry acting after all; for, when a few minutes later, my Lady made her way to his room, the stern, the unforgiving look had passed from his face, the imperious gesture was there no more. She found him with his proud head bowed between his hands, weeping as a strong, proud man alone can weep: weeping, it may have been, for what he deemed his dishonoured name—weeping, it may have been, for his blasted hopes, for his expectations never to be realized—weeping, it may have been, over the memory of days for ever passed away—weeping, it may have been, and, oh! God grant it, for the thought of the priceless love which he had so heedlessly trampled under foot, for the fair, young life on which he had thrown so fearful a blight—weeping, weeping, even for his lost, lost boy!

Whether he had been in earnest, or whether he had but been acting a part which he had forced himself to play, God alone can tell; but, of this I am quite sure, that there was no acting in the fierce gesture with which he threw my Lady's hand aside when she laid it on his arm; no acting in the bitter words with which he bade her leave him to himself; no acting in the weary, weary cry with which, when she had gone, he drew his little child once more to his breast, and sobbed, and wept, as if the very fountains of his heart were broken up; wept, as I think he would have wept in the days gone by, if it had been his lot to have had to lay in an early grave the fair-haired boy whom, in his pride and haughty rage, he had thus cast for ever from his heart and love.

CHAPTER XII.

FACE TO FACE.

At the conclusion of the unsatisfactory interview with Sir Percy, which I have recorded in the last chapter, I returned home utterly dispirited and cast down at the gloomy aspect which the affairs of poor Eustace but too certainly wore. I saw that, at least for the present, Sir Percy was quite implacable, and that any interference on behalf of his son would only widen the breach between them. I was equally convinced that should Eustace persevere in his determination to see his father, such a step would be productive of nothing but misery now, and but too probably lead to a final and complete rupture between them. On the other hand, I could not help hoping that if they could but be kept apart for some little time, until reason had again resumed her sway over the angry and chafed mind of Sir Percy, all might yet be well. At all events, and under every point of view, I deemed it simply my duty to inform my friend of the interview which I had had with his father, and its results; at the same time, pressing upon him more earnestly than ever my own conviction of the absolute madness of endeavouring to force himself upon Sir Percy, and beseeching him to listen to my advice and be guided by my counsels. He heard my story in silence, and made no effort to combat my arguments; but I was grieved beyond measure to see that the cloud only gathered more darkly than ever upon his brow, that the lines about his mouth grew harder and harder still, that the look of determination assumed a more fixed, I had almost said a more dogged, expression than before. When I had done, he laid his head upon the table for a second or two, then came over and shook me by the hand, and so, without a word, but with a world of sorrow and of stern resolve engraven on his poor, pale face, passed from out my sight.

He would not come down to dinner that day, but, to my very great astonishment, he came to me in the evening and asked me to accompany him for a walk. But too happy to witness even the slightest indication of anything that I might look upon as a return to a better and more cheerful state of mind, I gladly assented, never suspecting, even in the most remote manner, the snare into which he was about to lead me, or the resolution which he had formed. He took my arm and led me in the direction of Percy Grange, without, however, attempting to enter the grounds. I tried my best to engage him in cheerful conversation, but, to my sorrow and pain, I failed, failed signally, and the failure was all the more discouraging from the hopes which I had formed but a few moments before. Every now and then he sighed as if his very heart were broken, but his sorrow never found vent in words—the overburthened soul never found relief in tears; and, although once or twice he leant heavily against me as he rested on my arm, he quickly recovered himself, and led me on until we reached a kind of a rustic seat which had been hastily piled up in a recess of the wall which surrounded the grounds of Percy Grange. This seat was near one end of a narrow country lane which ran round a considerable portion of the Grange. It took a sharp turn just at this point, and the seat was so arranged that a person advancing from that corner would be upon the occupiers of it almost before they were aware of his approach. Upon this seat Eustace placed himself, whilst I threw myself on the sward at his feet, that I might be the better able to look up into his face, and win from him, if possible, one of those bright smiles which in days gone by had sat so frequently and so fittingly upon it. Now, however, it did not seem to be possible to win a cheerful word or a happy look from him. Several times, when he saw how much his conduct pained me, he tried, indeed, to smile and speak pleasantly to me; but he faltered and broke down with the half-formed word upon his quivering lips, and the sad smile which flitted for an instant across his face, like a gleam of sunshine playing over some scene of utter desolation and decay, was infinitely more painful to behold than the most passionate gush of tears could ever have been.

Thus we had sat for some little time, when, suddenly, the sound of a horse's hoofs fell upon my ear. The rider, whoever he might be, was evidently advancing at a leisurely pace upon us from the corner of the lane near which the seat, to which I have already alluded, was placed. As yet he was invisible to us, but, as the sounds came nearer and nearer, I marked that Eustace had become more deadly pale than ever, that the cold sweat was standing in thick drops upon his brow, and that he was trembling violently in every limb. Before I could rise to my feet Sir Percy Percy had ridden into the lane, and Eustace, with outstretched hands, and with a cry which sounded strangely on the quiet evening air, was rushing wildly towards him. In an instant, recovering from his surprise, Sir Percy reined in his horse, and turned as if he would ride away in the direction whence he had come. Before he could effect his purpose, Eustace had thrown himself upon the ground, and had got his arms twined fast about his father's feet. I heard a wild cry of Father, Father, rising from his lips in agonizing tones as he clung madly to the stirrup, and every instant I expected to see him trampled beneath the horse's hoofs. Although I was standing within a few yards of them, I thought it was no time for me to interfere; nay, I even dared to hope that, matters having come to this pass, the father's heart *must* of necessity relent at last. But the evil look which I had seen that morning passed once more across his face, only more fearfully, more hideously than ever. I think he uttered never a word, but turned away his head, and made strong and violent efforts to disengage himself from the clutch of his son. Once or twice the horse plunged wildly, but Eustace never relinquished his hold, never ceased that cry which might have pierced the heart of a stone, " Forgive me, Father! only forgive me, this is all I ask! Father! Father! Father!" and, still, I interfered not. A moment more, and with the look of a very devil, distorting and rendering hideous his noble face, I saw him raise himself in his stirrups. I saw him lift the wicked hand that held his heavy riding whip high above his head, and *then* I rushed in between them. The heavy whip came down with a crashing blow upon my head and shoulders, almost maddening me with pain, but I heeded it not. I had saved *him* from the cruel stripe. I had saved his father's hand from the deadly crime, and this was all I cared for. I knew well enough that he would not have struck me intentionally, and I could pardon him the rest. I hardly know what followed next. I heard him, even in the torrent of his rage, uttering some words of apology to me, but

I did not heed them. I threw myself upon him, snatched the whip from his hands, and flung it with all my strength over the hedge. Once more he rose in his stirrups and struck his spurs furiously into his horse. The beast plunged madly in the narrow lane, scattering the stones and dust in all directions. Then there was a loud cry, a cry louder and more heart-rending than ever, and I felt myself thrown violently on one side, so violently, indeed, that I staggered and fell, as Sir Percy Percy, his head uncovered, and his long hair floating in the wind, his eyes glaring like two unholy fires in the midst of his distorted face, rode past me as furiously as ever spur and voice could urge his frightened and excited beast. I was stunned for a moment or two by my fall, but I quickly recovered myself, and the first object which met my dazed sight was enough to recall me to myself in an instant. My friend lay stark and motionless before my eyes. As I knelt down, that, with a tender and a pitying hand, I might raise his head out of the dust which so defiled the golden glory of his long, fair hair, the crimson blood gushed out in torrents from his nostrils and his mouth—his head fell back as if it were a log of wood—his form grew stiff and rigid in my arms, and I was fain to lay him down once more among the dust and stones of the narrow country lane, fain to lay him down, to all appearance, stark and dead before my very eyes.

* * * * * * *

And thus they parted—Father and Son—never to look into each other's eyes again, except for one brief instant, till, on that dread day which is to make all things straight, they shall stand, face to face, before the judgment-seat of God.

END OF BOOK II.

BOOK THIRD.

BEATING TO THE SHORE.

"There is no flock, however watched and tended,
   But one dead lamb is there!
There is no fireside, howsoe'er defended,
   But has one vacant chair!

We will be patient, and assuage the feeling,
   We may not wholly stay;
By silence sanctifying, not concealing,
   The grief that must have way."

CHAPTER XIII.

BEATING TO THE SHORE.

WITH its never-ceasing ebb and flow, each wave drifting us nearer and nearer to the everlasting shores, the ocean of life for ever rolls along. Now, a million sun-lights dance upon its breast, and twinkle on its placid surface, till it seems to glow, a sea of silver, beneath the unclouded azure of the summer sky. Anon, that sky grows dark, and angry clouds roll up, each one fiercer and more threatening than the seething mass which the howling wind has just borne away upon its wings— till, at last, the foaming, boundless sea breaks out with one wild roar in all the majesty, the resistless fury, of the mighty storm. But, whether in the calm and sunny splendour of the summer's day, whether in the peace and still repose of the moonlit sky, or whether in the raging and the howling of the relentless storm, still it rolls along that ocean of our life, drifting us with its every wave nearer and nearer to the everlasting shores. Since I parted from you, courteous reader, I need scarcely say that the world has not stood still for me or for those whom I ventured to bring under your notice in the former part of this book. Years have rolled away since I held my friend in my arms in that narrow country lane—since, in the bitterness of a heart that was wrung to its inmost core, I laid him down, to all appearance, stark and dead. He sits before me as I pen these lines. Like myself, he has advanced a good way on the journey of his life. On the back of his chair, looking fondly down upon him, there leans a fair-haired youth, whose appearance carries me away at once some thirty years at least—to the days when his father and I were boys at Atherby school together. Sometimes, when I am wandering abstractedly about the house, as I have a habit of doing, and chance to come upon that youth unexpectedly, I am for the moment quite startled and carried out of myself. His resemblance to what his father was some thirty years ago, is so striking, the delusion is so perfect, that it is little wonder if, for a few seconds, I forget the intervening years, with all their trials and their cares; if, for a few seconds, I forget that my hand is resting on the shoulder of his father's son, and not on that of the Eustace Percy of thirty years ago. As I have just said, *he* sits before me as I write these lines. *He* lays his hand upon my arm and declares that I shall not pen another word until I have told you (these words are his, not mine) that if he sits before me this day, the honoured lord and master of Percy Grange, he owes it all to me and mine;

owes it all to me and mine that he lives (again, the words are his) to oblige me to tell the remainder of our story truthfully and to the full. As briefly, then, and as simply as may be, I will endeavour to relate what remains to be told of those whose fortunes have been brought before you in the pages of this book. If your kind interest in us, but most of all in *him*, has caused you to follow our fortunes thus far, I trust, as I believe, that the same kind interest will make you follow us, even to the end—will make you bear patiently with the little that is yet to be said. Before I can proceed, however, I must gather up my papers and hurry away to my own little room. I must have no more looking over my shoulder to see what I am writing. If he had seen much of what I have already penned, I am afraid that he would insist upon my destroying it. I am sure that he would not allow me to write much of what is yet to come, and as I am determined, spite of his humility and all his protestations to the contrary, to have my own way in this matter, my only chance is to keep my manuscript out of his sight until my work is done, until I can place the first copy of my book in the hands of him whose story it endeavours to tell; him whose Christian virtues and whose noble qualities it has striven to trace with an earnest and a loving, though it may be feeble, pen.

After that last interview with his father, at

which I merely glanced, and which I purposely softened down as much as possible, Eustace had a long and dangerous illness. I took him home and laid him in the best room which our humble cottage possessed. My mother tended him as if he had been her own, with a never-failing vigilance and love which endeared her to me, if that had been possible, a thousand times more deeply than ever. All the best and deepest sympathies of her motherly heart were enlisted to the full in favour of the poor, pale youth who lay upon our bed, an outcast from his father and his father's house, hovering for long and anxious weeks upon the very confines of the grave. Night and day, she or I was ever with him, that if, perchance, the closed eye should ever again open upon the world, its first glance of re-awakened life might fall upon a loving and a kindly face; that if, perchance, what we feared so much should come to pass, there might be a loving hand to wipe away the gathering sweats of death, to close the weary eye in its long, last sleep. For weeks it was doubtful whether he would ever rally from the fearful shock which had shaken his frame to its inmost nerve. When there was no longer any fear about his body, there was for some few days a more terrible fear still, the fear that his mind, at once so sensitive and so delicately attuned, so cruelly tried, and so terribly overwrought, might never recover its balance and its tone; and God alone knows how the hot tears rained down my face, how the sobs rose from my overcharged heart, when, one calm evening, after weeks of long and weary watching, he at last opened his eyes, and I saw that he knew me; knew that it was my hand that was bathing his brow; knew that they were my tears which were falling on his face; knew, after I had knelt down by the side of his bed, that it was my voice which was forcing its way in broken and in faltering accents, in tones that were trembling with very excess of loving thankfulness, to the throne of that God who had restored him to us. He recovered rapidly after this, for he was nursed by one whose motherly love and care went far to make him forget that, during all these weary weeks, the hand which above all others should have tended him with a never-flagging care had never wiped one drop of sweat from off his pallid brow; that the voice which should have been for ever raised in humble supplication for him to the throne of God had never taken the trouble to inquire whether he were still a dweller on the earth; that the proud heart which had vindicated its fancied rights at such a terrible cost had been consistent, even when the angel of death was glaring in all its horrors on his sight, consistent even to the very end.

Whilst watching by the bed of my friend, I had had time and opportunity enough to look into the future which lay open before me. Little by little, each day more and more clearly, that future seemed to resolve itself into a definite shape and form. Each day a path which I had never thought to tread, a path from which I shrunk back with fear and trembling, grew plainer and plainer still before my feet. At first, I thought that it was only a delusion and a snare in which the tempter was seeking to involve me. In all the fervour and simple devotion of my new-found faith, with all the ardour of a heart that had only just begun to taste and see how sweet God is to those who love him, I prayed for light and guidance in this all-important matter. The more I prayed the clearer grew that path; the greater my dread, the deeper my own conviction of my utter unworthiness to aspire to that holy vocation which, morning, noon, and night, was ever before my mind, ever urging itself upon me, ever seeming to ask for the sacrifice of myself and all that man may offer in humble adoration as a holocaust to his Lord and God; and, if I still hesitated and hung back, it was not, as my Master knows, that I grudged Him the heart which He seemed so earnestly to ask of me; but because I did not deem myself worthy to lay it at His blessed feet, because I did not deem myself fit to take upon me that burthen which angel's shoulders might fear to bear. It was my privilege and my consolation to enjoy, during this time of doubt and perplexity, a blessing which is found in its fulness and entirety in the Church of God alone, viz., the guidance and direction of a wise and saintly servant of the Most High. To him I laid bare the most hidden corner of my heart and soul. To him I made known that secret voice which, as I have just said, seemed, morning, noon, and night, to be whispering in my soul, to be asking me to sacrifice and devote myself to my Master's business. To him, in the sacred confidences which had birth as I knelt at his feet, that I might pour out the story of my sorrows and my doubts into his friendly breast, I laid open without reserve all my aspirations and all my fears; and, when he, in the name of his Master, bade me follow the footsteps of Him who had gone before me, teaching me that father, and mother, and all the world besides, are to be esteemed of less value than the dust beneath their feet by those who are called to toil in that whitening field where the harvest, indeed, is great but the labourers few, what could I do but throw myself upon my face before the sacred tabernacle in which His loving glory dwelleth, that I might pour out before Him the heart that was far too full for speech—that I might strive to cry aloud to Him, in such faltering words as my trembling lips could find, " Take, O Lord, take and receive my entire liberty, my memory, my understanding, and my whole will? Whatever I have and all that I possess Thou hast bestowed upon me. To

Thee I return it all, and surrender it all to be governed entirely by Thy will. Grant me only Thy grace and Thy love, and I am rich enough, nor do I desire anything more." What could I do but beg and beseech of Him to perfect and to finish the good work which His own right hand had so mercifully begun? What could I do but beg and implore of Him, as the choicest grace which He could give me, so to watch over and to protect me, so to keep his watchful and his loving hand ever upon me, that I might be, at least, a humble and a faithful, if not a profitable, servant in His holy vineyard,—that, through time and through eternity, I might be a holocaust laid upon the altar of His love, a holocaust to be consumed to the greater honour and glory of His adorable name?

I think I could not well have told you the story of my vocation in fewer words than I have done. If you deem that I could have done so, I beg of you to think those words unsaid. It was, after my conversion, the great grace of my life, a grace so immense and of such infinite import, to me at least, that, although, if I could pour out my whole being in one gushing act of thanksgiving I should still fall far short of what is due from me for such a gift, I would not willingly say one word more than is absolutely necessary about it; and it *was* necessary to my purpose to inform you of the fact.

For some little time I thought that Eustace

would have been drawn in a like direction. Naturally speaking, and if such should be the will of God, he was very anxious to enter the ecclesiastical state; but, in the mysterious designs of Providence, he, who was so infinitely my superior in everything that was holy and pure, was left to serve his God and save his soul in the midst of the world; whilst I was taken to co-operate in that most divine of all divine works, the salvation of immortal souls. It was the will of God that Eustace, living in the midst of the world, discharging its duties, and surrounded by its follies, should exhibit to that world the sublime picture of a Catholic and a Christian gentleman; the picture of one who knows how to use the things of the world, even in their abundance, without being contaminated by them; the picture of a gentleman, so perfect in its idea, so true and so complete in its verification, so bright and so radiant in its fair garment of Christian virtues and their heroic practice, that, many and many a time, I am fain to blush with shame, but a shame that is full of admiring love, as I think of the lessons of faith, and of sanctity, and of truth, which his life teaches to me, me who, infinitely less worthy as I was, was, nevertheless, called to a state so much more holy and perfect in itself than that in which he serves his God with such a faithful and an earnest care.

Thus my poor mother's wish that I should enter the Church was fulfilled, but in a way that she had little thought. It was another great blow to her, but she bore it like a loving and true-hearted woman, as she was. When I told her of it, after the first great burst of grief was over, she only drew me closer to herself, and strove to murmur through her tears, "Thy will be done, my God, Thy will, not mine, be done." Then a little while, and once again her arms were clinging to my neck, her mother's lips were pressed upon my brow, her mother's tears were raining down upon my face. Then once again, as she held me in what, perchance, might be a last embrace, forgetful of the great change which had come upon me, with all that such a change might well import; forgetful how her own long-cherished hopes, her expectations, nourished through so many weary years, had been scattered to the winds in what, under any other circumstances, would have been such a cruel way; forgetful of all except that she yet held me in her arms, that I was the only son of my mother and she a widow, all her mother's heart came gushing out upon me still once more; as still once more she clung about my neck, and sobbed and cried as though her very heart would break, "My child! my child! I had not thought of this, and God only knows how hard it is to bear—but, still, my child—oh, surely still, my darling, darling child!"

CHAPTER XIV.

LIGHT UPON THE WATERS.

* * * * * * *

ANOTHER period of some five years, and I have attained the summit of my hopes, and the object of my highest ambition. We are all living together, my mother, Eustace, and I, in a small country town some few miles from London, where I have been placed by my superior. Whilst these five years have been years of quiet, happiness, and almost undisturbed calm to me, it has been very different with poor Eustace. They have been years of searching trial, of anxious, weary care, to him. Whilst I can see the marks of them in his face and on his brow, I can read their effects still more plainly in every action of his daily life. Not a trial has passed over him which he has not turned to its account. Not a tribulation from which he has not derived its profit. The unrelenting anger, the unbending pride of Sir Percy, have but driven him into closer union with that Fatherly Heart which is ever alive to the wants and the necessities of even the humblest of His children; and he has experienced to the full with what a plentiful and an overflowing love the Lord taketh up those who are forsaken by father and mother for following His divine call.

Eustace has never seen his father since they parted after that dreadful interview in the narrow, country lane. Whenever he has called at his father's house, and acting under a strong sense of duty, he has several times done so, he has been rigorously denied admittance. When, acting under that same sense of duty, he has written to his father, his letters have been invariably returned with a bitter and unforgiving message scrawled upon the back of them. It has been a heavy trial, a trial such as a sensitive and delicate nature like his feels in its most touching poignancy; but it has only taught him to draw nearer, as I have just said, to his heavenly Father, has only filled his affectionate soul with a more tender compassion and with a greater yearning towards the earthly parent who has cast him off, and who has thus hardened his heart, or allowed it to be hardened, against his child; has only caused him to pray with an ever-increasing fervour and earnestness that God, in His own good time, may deign to soften that poor father's heart.

It has been a hard struggle with him, too, to earn his daily bread. Before I left England, in order to complete my studies, I had a long and anxious conversation with my mother about the future of Eustace. The result was that, acting under her advice, I positively refused to stir until Eustace had promised us to take up his abode beneath her roof. Perceiving, instinctively, that Percymoate was no place for him to live in, she declared that she had already made up her mind to leave it, and that nothing should induce her to change this determination. Poor Eustace tried to resist for some little time, but when he perceived how fully my mind was made up not to stir until he had acceded to our wish, and that he was hindering me from pursuing the course marked out for me, with many expressions of ardent gratitude, with many tears of loving thankfulness, he consented to do what we asked of him. But here his complaisance ended. Yes, he would live with my mother, he said, and to the latest hour of his life, would thank us for allowing him to do so; but it was only on one condition, viz., that he contributed his full share to the household expenses. He could not consent to be a burthen, so he put it, even upon us. His own hand must earn his daily bread. This was a point on which, of course, we could not press him—on which we could make no conditions but such as his high spirit and his independent nature suggested; and yet, poor fellow, how was he to earn his daily bread? How was he, so delicately nurtured,—he who had been watched with such tender care, lest the winds of heaven might blow too roughly upon his cheek, to earn his bread by the sweat of his brow, or the work of his hand? How was he to face the world with its bitter sneers, with its heartless pity, with its scathing cynicism? How was he to haggle and bargain with the heartless crew who would bind him down to the last farthing; who would wring the last drop of blood out of his frame rather than lose the value of a mite by him? How were they to understand his gentle nature, his noble instincts, his delicate sympathies; and yet, it was with such as these that he must haggle and bargain, and fight for the pittance that was to purchase that daily bread which he would not consent to share with us, and which, dearly as we loved him, and highly as we prized him, we could not wrong his noble nature by pressing upon him in such cruel circumstances. As I thought of all these things—thought of all that had been, all that was, and all that was to be—thought (and this was the bitterest reflection of all) how powerless I was to help him—how utterly impotent to pluck one thorn from off his rugged path; what could I do but, in the fervour and keenness of my sympathy, my intense compassion for him, pray with all the yearning pity of my soul that my God, in His merciful goodness, might temper the biting winds to the poor shorn lamb!

Before I started for the continent I saw my mother and Eustace fairly settled in London, where she, for reasons well known to herself and to me, had determined to take up her abode. During the five years I was away from them Eustace never left her. Although he had adhered with inflexible firmness to his resolution to contribute his fair share to the household expenses, I need scarcely say that my dear mother had the means, as she most certainly had the desire, of making him much more 'happy and more comfortable than he could have been in any other circumstances. I trust that none of my readers have ever experienced such an ordeal as that through which poor Eustace Percy passed during these few years of trial and of painful toil. Unless they had passed through such an ordeal, I am quite certain that they could never realize it, or comprehend its significance and its terrible import. Imagine yourself reared in the midst of wealth and splendour, surrounded by everything that is beautiful in nature and art, your every want not merely supplied but anticipated by the watchful hands which wait upon your slightest wish, the wish which to them is a command and a law. Imagine yourself brought up to no trade or profession which will enable you to earn as much bread as will keep the very breath in your body. Imagine that you, thus delicately reared, thus tenderly nursed; you, who have been endowed by nature with the most lively sensibilities, the most exquisite perception of everything that is noble, and holy, and true—are suddenly thrown out of house and home, and cast upon a world that is as strange to you as you are an object of pity, even

of contempt, to it, that you may earn your daily
bread along its highways, and in its streets; that
you may snatch your miserable pittance in the
fierce struggle which is ever seething within its
breast, and tell me, do you believe that your lot
will be a happy or a pleasant one? Think of the
sneering upstart who will ask no higher gratification than that of grinding your dainty mawkish-
ness, as he will style it, under his feet! Think of
the low-bred arrogance with which he will flaunt in
your face the wealth which *he* knows not how to
use, the luxury in which *he* can only wallow!
Listen to the stinging sneer with which he will
tell to the herd that fawn about him the story
of your poverty and your fall, and as you listen,
turn away your weary head, not in shame, but in
sorrow, and hide it where you may! Sprinkle the
ashes over your brow—let your tears roll on un-
checked—turn your face to the wall, and in the
silence of the midnight hour, when none but He
may hear, cry aloud to God in the bitterness of
your bruised heart, for, so far as I know, you have
no comfort to expect from man, no soothing balm
to look for from mortal hand! Think of the coarse
task-master who will dole out to you with a grudg-
ing hand, perhaps with a curse, the miserable
pittance which you have so hardly earned with
the sweat of your aching brow, the pittance
which scarcely keeps your body and your soul
together in mortal coil! As you take it in the

poverty that is so timid and so fearful, the poverty that would be so abject were it less holy in its cause or less patient in its endurance, think of the plentiful profusion of your father's house, from which you are a more utter outcast than if you were the veriest prodigal who ever squandered a father's substance in debauchery and riotous living! Think of the brother's hand you may not press, the sister's lip you may not kiss! Think of those who, in the day of your prosperity, followed your steps with such cringing servility, scattering the false and the noxious flowers of their flattery before your feet, and who, after battening upon your substance as long as a shred of that substance lasted, now pass you in the public street as if they had never seen your face before, with a look of well-bred indifference or of silent contempt! Think of the long and the weary nights, think of the days longer and more weary still! Think of your threadbare coat and your worn-out shoes! Think of the biting cold of the winter's frost, the pitiless pelting of the winter's rain! Think of the gnawing hunger which even you, who were clad in fine linen and who fared sumptuously every day, are constrained to feel in all its sharpness, in all its bitter pangs! Think of these things, for, I tell you, they are realities, that they have place in the very midst of us, and that men suffer them for conscience sake even in the nineteenth century. Imagine that such a lot had been yours. Imagine it going on, day after day, and week after week, and month after month, and year after year, till it seems as if nature can bear no more, and then tell me whether, if you were not restrained by the saving thought of God, and the undefined dread of that which is to come, you would not be tempted to throw away, as a thing not worth the having, that life which you hold as a sacred deposit to be returned to your Maker's hand—tell me whether, if it were not for the blessed hope of the better things which are in store, if it were not for the blessed expectation of the day which is to set all these things straight, you would not turn your weary face to the wall, —you would not, in the despairing agony of a heart broken in its struggle with the world, like Job of old, curse the day on which you saw the light,—you would not be like to those who look for death and it cometh not, who dig as for a treasure, and who rejoice exceedingly when they have found the grave.

Through such an ordeal as that which I have attempted to sketch in feeble words, an ordeal which no mortal pen, much less such a pen as mine, can ever adequately describe, did my poor friend Eustace Percy wend his weary way for many a year, his path uncheered by a single ray of light, except such as was cast upon it by his own unclouded faith, his own unwavering hope, his own illimitable, never-changing love. What my mother's hand, my mother's love could do for him, was done even as if it would have been for me; but, at the most, it was but a solitary gleam, rendering the surrounding gloom all the darker and more hideous. Earning his daily bread, as he was constrained to do, now by giving lessons to the children of those whom he could persuade to employ him, now by working for such miserable pittances as he could occasionally earn from a London publisher,—what wonder, if, returning full of health and spirits to my native land, I was inexpressibly shocked at the change in his appearance —what wonder if all the bounding gladness, all the eager joyfulness with which I had rushed into his presence, faded away from me as I held him in my arms, as I looked into his poor pale face, as I marked the lines along his brow, the faded lustre of his eye, the dishevelled confusion of his golden hair! What wonder if, as he strove to throw himself at my feet, that he might kiss the hands that had been consecrated for the work of God, I could but raise him in my arms, I could but fold him to my breast, I could but weep in speechless agony over what seemed to be the wreck of such a glorious promise, I could but vow in my inmost heart, the heart which could find no words, that, to the latest hour of my life, I would devote that life to the service of him who was dear above all price to me, dearer than ever now when I saw how much he stood in need, not only of my love, but of my constant watchfulness and care—him whom I loved in God with all the depth and the purity of a brother's unsuspecting love, whom I loved even as David loved Jonathan—him who had been the companion of my youth and the friend of my riper years, but whom I had never known except as the same brave, true, honest, pure, single-hearted man—him at whom I had been proud to look with admiring love as, in the generous instincts of his holy soul, he had sacrificed all things else that he might purchase the pearl of great price, the pearl which he had purchased at a cost which few besides himself would ever have had the courage to pay!

For some time after my return no one can tell how deep a source of pain and anxiety Eustace was to me. We did our best, without boasting I may say that we did our very best, to lighten his troubles, to cheer his path, to persuade him to relax his labours, and share our humble fare. I think he could scarcely have realized how much I was grieved, and how deep was my pain, or he would not have been so inflexible as he was. His cheek grew paler every day, and there was a period when I trembled as I thought that I saw the hand of death already upon him, but God spared us this trial. Several times, as he sat opposite to me in my little study, looking so pale and wan, so utterly worn and broken with his self-imposed labours and toil, I could not resist the impulse to rise from my chair and go over to his side, to put my arm round his shoulder, and whisper in his ear, "It is a hard trial, Eustace, my poor fellow; God knows it is a hard trial. May He give you the strength which can come from His hand alone." As he felt the tears which I could not control falling upon his brow he raised his face to mine, with the simple, childlike look of other and far happier days beaming in his eyes, but this was all. It was ever the same. I had never thoroughly understood him, and I think I understood him less than ever now, when he had attained heights of sanctity and perfection which I had never reached, to which, perhaps, I had never even aspired. In the guileless innocence of a heart that had learnt to trust God, as entirely and as confidingly, as lovingly and as truly, when it was engulphed in an ocean of sorrow as when it was surrounded by the excess of joy and of consolation, he was walking a path which but few are called upon to tread, and he was striving to walk it, even as his Master had done before him, without a complaining word, without a repining thought, without a desire to lay aside, even for one day, until it might be that Master's will, the crown of thorns that was pressed upon his brow, or the cross that was laid upon his shoulders; without the wish to remove from his path a single one of the briars which so cruelly mangled his torn and bleeding feet.

As I have just said, I never thoroughly understood or penetrated the depths of that holy and that loving heart. Every day that I spent with him taught me more and more of its sanctity and its love, its perfect conformity to the adorable will of God. He was, at this time, with the true instinct of holiness, most reserved in speaking of himself, most unwilling to refer, even in the most distant manner, to his trials or his cares. One evening, however, and I remember it well, I could not help showing more than my usual anxiety about him. I could not help manifesting, more than I was accustomed to do, the loving solicitude which was ever welling up in my heart for his dear sake. As he marked the troubled expression of my face, and the tears which, spite of all my efforts, rolled down my cheek, he rose from his chair, and, coming over to where I sat, knelt down at my feet. As he raised his face I was struck more than I can well say with the expression that was written in its every feature. There was a flush upon his cheek which I had not seen there for many a day, and his eyes were all on fire with a light which was not of the earth. I felt instinctively that I was in the presence of one whose heart was very near to God. As with a feeling that had as much of reverence as of love in it, I bowed my head to him as he knelt at my feet, he put out his hand, and drew my face down so that he could whisper to me. The tones of his voice were ineffably solemn and sweet as they fell upon my ear; as, in the silent stillness of the evening's calm, he murmured to me the lesson of comfort and of consolation which he himself had learnt so deeply and so well.

"*Why, then, art thou afraid to take up thy Cross, which leadeth to a kingdom?*

"*In the Cross is salvation: in the Cross is life: in the Cross is protection from all thy enemies.*

"*There is no health of the soul, nor hope of eternal life, but in the Cross.*

"*Take up, therefore, thy Cross, and follow Jesus, and thou shalt go into life everlasting.*

"*He is gone before thee carrying His Cross, and He died for thee upon the Cross, that thou mayest also bear thy Cross, and love to die upon the Cross.*

"*Because if thou die with Him, thou shalt also live with Him; and if thou art His companion in suffering thou shalt also partake in His glory.*

"*Go where thou wilt, seek what thou wilt, and thou shalt not find a higher way above, nor a safer way below, than* THE WAY OF THE HOLY CROSS."

As the tones of his voice seemed to melt away, I bent my head to him more lowly and more reverently still. When I looked up I found that he had gone. It was but a short lesson, yet it was one which taught me much. It revealed to me many things in that holy soul which, up to this, had been more or less mysterious to me. It taught me more clearly than, perhaps, I had ever known it before, how the Heart of God can work upon the heart of his creature; how It can draw the human heart to Itself; how It can transform the jagged thorns into fairest flowers; how It can clear away from the toilsome path the cruel stones which so beset the bleeding feet; how It can wipe the tear of sorrow from the weeping eye; how It can cheer and raise the drooping soul; how It can fill to utter overflowing with the fire of its heaven-born love the poor human heart that, in its honest simplicity, in its loving truth, has learnt what it is to do all and to dare all for its Leader and its God.

Truly the clouds hung dark and lowering over the stormy waves, but there was light upon the waters, nevertheless, even the blessed light of God; the light that shone with never-fading ray, pointing the weary heart to the happy and the peaceful shores, which grew nearer and more plain with every passing day.

CHAPTER XV.

COMING RIGHT.

AND now, before I bring this simple narrative to a close, I must return for a few moments to the history of one whom I introduced to the notice of my reader in my introductory pages, but whose name, for various reasons, I have not since mentioned. Poor Tom Bowman! Were it not that my little history would be incomplete without it, I would fain pass his story by with a silent tear, with a sigh of regret for the life that was thrown away, for the noble faculties and the generous instincts that were wasted on frivolous or unworthy objects. It was poor Tom's misfortune to find himself, in early life, placed in that unfortunate position in which a man may say of himself that he is "Lord of himself, that heritage of woe." Young, rich, and handsome; with passions within his breast that were fearfully strong for good or for evil; with no father's authority to restrain him; no father's voice to pour sage words of loving counsel into his deluded ear; with all the false glitter, all the seducing glare of the world appealing to him in its most attractive forms; with that same world fawning about his feet and spreading its fairest flowers upon his path, what wonder if poor Tom, spite of all his naturally good dispositions, his noble qualities, his open, generous heart, did but enter upon the great journey that was before him, the ocean of life, to be drifted full sail to shipwreck, as utter as it was speedy, as hopeless as it was complete?

Such histories, the histories of faculties abused, and of talents thrown away; of young lives wasted, aye, and worse than wasted; of noble affections and of generous sympathies misspent upon objects from which they should have shrunk in loathing disgust, are surely ineffably painful; yet, alas, they are but too true and too common, and the pen that would fain pass them by, would fain cover them over with a loving, if, perchance, a partial gloss, is constrained to write them down in simple and in earnest truth, that all who run may read; that all may learn that the life which is not devoted to duty is thrown away; that all may know that the path of duty, duty animated and enlivened by faith, is before the feet of every man, no matter how young, how rich, or how heedless he may be; that all may know that it is the path of duty, and not of inclination, which leads to happiness here, and to something which is more than happiness in the better land beyond the everlasting shores.

And, hence, dear Tom, if with a loving pen,

with a pen that shall touch as lightly as may be on thy failings, that shall extol to the utmost the noble qualities with which thy generous heart ran over, I venture to write in a few simple words the record of thy life, surely, oh, surely, it is not that I may bring that poor, wasted life of thine in undue prominence before the world; not that I may say one word of thee which may be unbecoming or unworthy of the trusting love, the boundless confidence, thou didst ever repose in him whose hand pens, with a love which few, perhaps, may guess, what *may* be the story of a wasted life, but what shall *surely* be the best tribute to thy memory which his hand can pay. So long as the world is what it is, so long will there be sad stories, like to thine, to be told. May there always be a tender voice to tell the tale, a gentle hand to deal lightly with the sad history of human weakness and of human sorrow! May there be always those who can think and who can act as the poet sings—

> " And when
> I speak of such among the flock as swerved
> Or fell, those only shall be singled out
> Upon whose lapse, or error, something more
> Than brotherly forgiveness may attend."

If thine was one of these sad tales, it was a tale that was not all dark, all gloomy, all without hope, without many a bright, many a redeeming trait. At its worst it is but a tale of an aimless life, of broken purposes, of aspirations unfulfilled, of keen affections wasted and thrown away—of generous instincts, worked upon by designing hands, perverted and abused. Whatever there was of foolishness, of indiscretion, and, it may have been, of sin, in thy poor life, has been weighed in the balance and has been judged long ere this. I believe in my very heart that the divine hand of Him whose mercies are above all His works, hath long since washed thee in His cleansing blood, hath long since clothed thee in the robe of His loving and His gracious condonation, hath long since made thy ransomed soul whiter than the driven snow; and if this be so, what mortal tongue shall dare to pass a harsher sentence on thee than that which thy Maker's gentle voice hath already spoken? But if all the world were with brazen tongue to pass its judgment on thy follies and thy weakness, it would still be mine—oh, surely, it would still be mine, to cover that folly with the veil of my love, a love which is none the less pure because it is faithful and true, none the less true because it knows how to palliate and to excuse.

I have already given you some slight idea of the manner of life which Tom Bowman led at Oxford. I have told you that he was the leader in everything that was noisy and out of order; but when I say this, do not suppose that I mean to assert that he was guilty of habitual excess of any kind. He was so full of health and animal spirits that a certain amount of noisy amusement seemed to be almost a necessity to him. Considering the companions into whose society he had fallen, and the large sums of money he always had at his command, it is not very wonderful if those amusements sometimes went beyond all due bounds, and degenerated into riot and disorder. Hence, although as I have just said, I do not think he was ever guilty of great or habitual excess; the whole tenor of his life was such as to compromise him seriously with the authorities; and some time before Eustace and I left Oxford, Tom had been requested, in terms which admitted of no demur, to withdraw from the University. I need scarcely say that it had pained me much to see poor Tom leading such a reckless, aimless life. It was very painful to see such fine talents as he undoubtedly possessed, thrown away and wasted; more painful still to witness his noble qualities, both of mind and heart, perverted and turned aside to unworthy or unbecoming objects. Poor Tom was afloat on the ocean of life with almost everything in his favour; with youth, health, riches, brilliant prospects, to waft him prosperously on the great journey. Unfortunately, he was unprovided with the rudder of fixed religious principles—religion and duty were words which had no defined and practical meaning in his regard—self-restraint and Christian abnegation were terms which had no recognised value in his vocabulary. The world, pleasure, self-gratification, were naturally enough the leading ideas in his mind, the leading objects for which he lived; and hence, the noble qualities with which his Maker had so liberally endowed him, did but help, through their abuse, to drift him all the more rapidly, all the more hopelessly, to the fatal rocks of ruin and destruction. I believe that I had more influence than any one else over Tom, but at this period my influence was very small, next to nothing, so far as practical results were concerned. When I remonstrated with him, and relying upon our old and firm friendship, I often did so with all the earnestness at my command; he listened to me patiently and quietly, but he always laughed my remonstrances off, and that in such a light-hearted, careless way that, spite of my annoyance, I could not be angry with him. Once or twice, indeed, when he had got himself into deeper trouble than usual with the authorities, and I pointed out to him in strong, blunt words, what must be the inevitable end of such a course as that on which he had entered, he seemed to appreciate the truth of what I said. He admitted that he was leading a very reckless and a very useless life; he promised me faithfully to reform and to embrace some profession, if it was only to keep himself out of mischief; but, alas! in two or three days it was just the same as before; and what wonder! A reformation without religion, a change of life arising from merely natural motives, having neither its beginning nor its end in the holy love of God, what is it but a house built upon the sands, a house to be rooted up and swept away from its very foundations by the first angry wave of passion and of sin which shall rise in the day of the storm against it?

I have just said that he had left Oxford some time before Eustace and I were received into the Church. He was abroad at the precise time, but when he heard of it he wrote at once in his old, off-hand style, offering me any assistance in his power. I need scarcely say that, whilst I declined his offer of assistance, I felt his good-natured kindness very truly and very deeply. I was still more deeply touched by one remark which his letter contained—a remark which might have been penned without a moment's thought, but which *might*, on the other hand, be the reflection of what was really passing in his mind, and which, if this should be so, afforded me strong grounds for hoping that he was not past all redemption:—" If you and Eustace Percy," he wrote, " felt that you ought to become Catholics, you have done right in following your convictions, and I honour you for it with all my heart and soul. You are two brave fellows. Would to God," he continued, " I could follow your example. Do you remember what I told you in the play-ground at Atherby school that Sunday when the Rector preached his no-Popery sermon? Who would have thought that you two would have become Catholics, while I have been going on from bad to worse, till I often think that I am past all hope? I have only one consolation," he went on, "and it is that my poor mother has not lived to see how utterly lost I have become, how miserably and how utterly I have broken every promise which I made to her in the days of my childish innocence. It is not often I pray now," he concluded in the same desponding and despairing way, " but when I heard what you had done, I *did* go down on my knees, and beg of God, as well as I knew how, to bless you two brave fellows, and I hope that He will do it; but as for me I become more and more convinced every day that I shall never come to any good. God help me, and have pity on me."

It was very pitiable to have him writing in this style, but there was a ray of consolation even in the miserable words which I have repeated, inasmuch as they showed that he was not utterly lost to a sense of his position and of his wretched state.

I never saw him during the period that I was abroad completing my studies. He wrote to me at irregular intervals, but always in the same reckless style; always with the same sad story to tell, the story of his poor, aimless, wasted life.

I think it was about two months after my return that, one morning, without further notice, he threw open the door of the room in which I was sitting, and caught me in his arms. I was delighted beyond measure to see him once again, for spite of all his follies and his weakness, I loved him really and truly; loved him, if not more deeply, perhaps more tenderly and compassionately, on account of that very weakness and that very folly. When I had recovered from my surprise, and had time to look him quietly in the face, I was inexpressibly shocked at the change in his appearance. He was as handsome as ever —his dress and his every movement bespoke the perfect and the finished gentleman, but there was a worn and weary look about his face, and more especially in his eyes, which gave the lie sadly to the light and almost flippant words with which he parried my questions,—a look which told of a heart ill at ease, of a heart to which all his wealth, all his so-called pleasures, all his so-called enjoyments, brought not one moment of real happiness or joy. How ill at ease was that poor heart became but too evident ere he had been half an hour in my company; for, when, with a freedom which was warranted by our long and intimate friendship, I began to press him on the subject of the life which he was leading; when I began to speak to him in hot and burning words which rose straight from my heart of the inevitable end of all this which must come sooner or later; when, in virtue of the sacred character with which I was clothed, I dared to speak to him in words of solemn authority and of stern rebuke; when I besought him in the name and for the dear sake of Him who had died for us both, to think of himself ere it was too late, the flippant words all faded away from his tongue, the worn and weary look grew deeper and deeper on his poor, pale face, the light faded more and more sadly out of his large, dark eyes, as, with a despairing cry, a cry which pierced my soul to its inmost core with sorrowful compassion for the young life that had been so wasted and so thrown away, he turned aside his head, and laid it on the back of a chair that he might hide from me the tears which he could not control, and which he was ashamed that I should see.

I let him weep a little while, and then I did my best to comfort and console him. Above all, I did my best to lead him to better and more holy things. Again he promised me earnestly, and, I believe, sincerely, and again he went his way and forgot his promise, or, to speak more correctly, was unfaithful to it. The appointed time had not come as yet. As yet, his resolutions were only built upon his own poor, wavering will; and, hence, as yet, they were utterly rooted up, and swept away by the first assault of the raging storm when it arose in its restless fury; as yet, I and those who loved him well could only watch him from a distance, and humbly pray for those better and those holier things, whose advent we could not descry through what appeared the ever-thickening gloom which gathered round his steps.

I did not see much of him after the interview which I have just described, and, to tell the truth, I could scarcely regret it. I found myself powerless to work any permanent change in him, and it was so painful to me to look upon his wasting form and to know as I did but too well that he was throwing himself away, body and soul, for time and eternity, utterly and hopelessly, unless God should interpose and work the change which His right hand alone seemed able to effect, that it was a positive relief not to see him at all. It was, as well as I remember, about nine months after my return that he came to my lodgings rather late one night. He appeared to me to look wretchedly ill and nervous, and excitable to a degree which I had never before witnessed. He only laughed, however, at my anxious words, and I found that he had come to make me promise to go on the morrow to witness a rowing match on the river, in which he was to take a prominent part, to pull the stroke oar, I think he expressed it. It was a matter in which, naturally speaking, I did not take the slightest interest. Moreover, I was very much engaged with my duties, but he pressed me so earnestly, and seemed so anxious about it, that, to please him, I promised to go. On the morrow I went, agreeably to my promise, and found large crowds of people assembled on the banks of the river where the match was to come off. Poor Tom seemed greatly delighted that I had kept my promise to him, and was in high spirits. He remained with me until it was time for him to go and take his place in the boat. As he left me he seemed so much excited that I begged of him earnestly to try and calm himself. "All right," he cried, as he turned away; "keep your eye on the red, and see how gloriously we'll beat them."

He went his way, and, instead of keeping my eye on the red, his colour, I became so absorbed in my melancholy reflections concerning him and his poor life, that I had forgotten all about the race until I was recalled to myself by the shouts of the crowd who were pressing along the banks of the river. As a louder shout than usual fell upon my ear, I raised my eyes and I saw that a most exciting race was taking place. The three boats were close abreast, and it seemed impossible to predict which would carry off the prize. Thus they rowed for some hundreds of yards or so, with no perceptible change in their relative positions. They were only about fifty yards from the goal when, with a bound which seemed to lift her fairly out of the water, Tom's boat shot ahead. Two or three vigorous strokes more, and, amid the frantic shouts of the enthusiastic crowd, she passed the post, winning by half her own length. Almost immediately after, it struck me that there was great noise and confusion among the crowd, but, for a moment or two, I did not heed it, thinking that it was nothing more than the excitement resulting from the race. Presently, I remarked them thronging round the place where the boats had stopped, but, still, I did not heed it. A second or two more, and there were loud cries for a doctor. Then I knew at once that there was something wrong, and I made my way, not without great difficulty, to where I saw the throng was thickest. Men were running hither and thither in a wild, excited way, whilst cries for a doctor rose on all sides. I don't know how it was, but I seemed to guess instinctively what had happened, and when the crowd saw my pale scared face they made way for me to pass. I was there in a second, and in that same second I took it all in. Four men were lifting poor Tom carefully out of the boat. He was ghastly pale, his eyes closed, and the blood gushing in torrents from his mouth. I thought he was already dead, but, as I rushed madly to his side, he opened his eyes, and his glance fell upon the well-known face. He knew me at once, and with a sad smile, which might have gone, I think, to a heart of stone, he tried to lift up his arms to me. They fell powerless at his side, but I knew what he would have. I motioned to them to place him gently on the ground, and then I sat down by his side. They laid his poor drooping head upon my breast. As I took him in my arms, he opened his glazing eyes once again, and fixed them on me with a longing and imploring look—a look which begged me more plainly and more touchingly than any words which fall from human lips could ever have done, not to leave him till the closing scene had come. I whispered in his ear, but that ear was closed to human voice. Although it was not so, I thought he was already dead; but God spared him to me for a little while, spared him in that mercy which came to him even in the eleventh hour. And so, as soon as might be, I carried my poor shattered wreck to my sorrowful home, and laid him on the bed from which he never rose again—thankful, even to my heart's inmost core, that it might be mine to tend him to the end; mine to smooth his passage to his early grave; mine the blessed and the holy privilege, a privilege which I would not have bartered for a monarch's crown, to lead that poor, wandering lamb to its loving Shepherd's feet; mine the blessed lot to bring eternal hope, and rest, and peace to that poor yearning soul.

I cannot write much more about it. He had broken a blood-vessel, and he never rallied. He seemed to make no effort, no struggle for life, but sank at once into a hopeless decline. I have spoken freely of his follies and his weakness; let me now, not only in love, but in common justice, speak of his repentance. I have seen many men die, and I have attended many dying beds, but I have attended none where the triumph of religion and of faith was more gloriously manifested than at that of poor Tom Bowman. He lingered several months, but, from the day I carried him home, his whole energies were turned to preparing to meet his God. He seemed to forget the world as completely as if he had never mixed in its follies, or been carried away by its deluding snares. His lost prospects, the riches which were now no more to him than the dust beneath his feet, nay, even the young life which was gliding so rapidly but inevitably away, seemed to give him no more concern than the wind which blew upon his flushed and fevered brow. Influenced as much by my own feelings as by that wordless but most touching appeal which I had seen in his eyes as he fell into my arms, I had carried him to our little cottage, and again my mother's benevolence had full scope for its exercise. Through the three months that God left him with us, I can safely say that nothing which affectionate solicitude, or never-flagging care could suggest, was wanting to him. Night and day, Eustace, my mother, or I, was ever at his side, so that there might ever be a friendly hand for his to clasp, a loving eye to meet his own, a careful and a tender touch to wipe away the sweats that gathered on his brow; and never did his eye meet ours but it told the same unvarying tale of grateful thankfulness, of patient resignation, of deepest hope and trust in God. It seemed as if all the intervening years had been swept away at one stroke, and as if the grace of his baptism had revived in all the brightness of its heaven-descended origin. Perhaps his mother, the mother who had trained the first aspirings of his heart to God, the mother who had taught him those early lessons which had been so sadly forgotten in the years of his folly, was praying for him before the throne of grace, and, by her prayers, had wrought this wonderful change. Who can tell? Only God. I was anxious to bring one of my brother clergymen to attend him, but he would not hear of it; he would receive no ministrations but mine. Of my relations with him in that capacity I may say no more than that they were of such a nature as to fill my heart to utter overflowing with burning thankfulness to God, who had so washed and purified that poor soul in the cleansing bath of His own most precious blood—of such a nature as to make me sob and cry aloud with very joy—of such a nature as to intensify a thousand-fold, if that had been possible, my wondering admiration of that holy Catholic faith, that noblest work of God, which can thus triumph over sin and death, which can cause men, even in their life's young spring, to go forth with as much cheerful joy to meet the heavenly Bridegroom, as fills the heart of the new-made bride on the day of her espousals.

And thus, day by day, and hour by hour, he faded away before our watchful eyes. I was sitting by his side one evening, little thinking that the end was so near at hand. I had given him the holy communion that morning; and, although he had been very ill and restless all the day, he seemed somewhat easier towards night. As I sat by the side of his bed, but drawn a little back, I could see his lips moving in prayer, although he was too weak to use the beads which were twined about his fingers. Suddenly, he made a motion to me to raise him up a little. I thought it might give him some relief, and so I took him in my arms and laid his head upon my breast. "Ambrose," he said to me all at once, and with a strange yearning earnestness in his voice, "Ambrose, I think it has been all a mistake, a weary, sad mistake; but, please God, it is coming right at last."

At the moment, I did not understand him or divine his meaning. "What has been all a mistake, Tom, my dear fellow?" I asked in astonishment.

He raised his eyes and looked me wistfully in the face. "Oh, this poor, wasted life of mine," he answered. "It has been all a sad mistake; but, Ambrose, dear Ambrose," he cried in eager accents, "do you think it is coming right at last? Oh, do you think it is coming right at last?"

I could scarcely answer him for the great sobs which were choking me, but, somehow, I managed to falter through my tears, "Yes, Tom, my dear, dear fellow, it is fast coming right. God knows it is surely coming right."

All at once his arms let go their hold, and his head fell back. As I laid him hastily down I caught one last look of his glazing eyes. I had just time to raise my hand once more in fervent blessing over him ere the solemn shadow passed across his face; and, then, I closed with a reverent touch the bright, dark eyes that had looked their last upon the world, and fell upon my knees to pray for the ransomed soul which had at length, as I humbly hoped and believed, entered into its everlasting rest.

Dear Tom Bowman, happier ten thousand times in thy death than in thy life, farewell to thee! Farewell to thee, till the happy day when, please God, we shall meet once more in that better land, where there shall be no more weeping or tribulation, no more sorrow or pain. I have told thy story because I believe that thou wouldst have wished me to tell it—that all who run may read —that all who read may take warning from thy poor, lost life—may learn that the only path which can lead to happiness is the path of duty and of truth. I trust that I have told that story tenderly —I know that I have told it lovingly. Farewell to thee, dear old friend, a long farewell!

CHAPTER XVI.

BEYOND THE EVERLASTING SHORES.

There is a homely proverb to the effect, as well as I remember, that it seldom rains but it pours, and it certainly seemed to be about to be verified in my case at this period. It was little more than a dozen years since Eustace Percy, Tom Bowman, and I, had made our boyish promise of eternal friendship, and already I had laid one of the three in an early grave, whilst I began to fear once more that it would not be long ere I should have the same sad office to perform for another of the trio. Soon after the death of poor Tom I began again to grow very uneasy about Eustace. In spite of all our efforts, all our entreaties, he still persevered in leading the same life of wearing and unflagging toil, but it was very evident to me that it could not last much longer. Sir Percy was as unforgiving as ever, and Eustace, inasmuch as he would not consent to share our pittance, was, consequently, altogether dependent upon his own exertions for his support. The nearest approach to a serious misunderstanding which ever arose between us was on this matter; but he was inflexible: and, as I have already said, it was a point of extreme delicacy, and one on which it was very difficult for me to urge him. I also discovered, accidentally, that he was supporting, and this out of his own hard earnings, several poor old people in the neighbourhood. When I remonstrated with him on this subject, and tried to show him that it was more than God expected from him, he silenced me with an argument which I will not repeat, but which brought the blush to my cheek, and made me turn away in silent, but in loving and admiring confusion. And thus, a bright and beautiful example of every Christian virtue, he toiled along the way which he had chosen, the royal way of the cross, turning neither to the right nor to the left, till he should have reached the appointed end. In the bitterness of my grief I was compelled to confess that, unless God should interpose in some way, which I did not foresee, to bring the troubles and the labours of my poor friend to a speedy and a happy close, this end was not very far distant. It was nearer than I thought, and after the sorrow and pain which immediately accompanied it had passed away, happier and more peaceful than I had ever dared to expect.

I was sitting in my little study one morning after breakfast. Eustace was opposite to me, preparing himself for his day's labour by going over some of those drudging lessons which he would persist in giving. As I glanced every now and then over the top of my newspaper at him, I thought I had never seen him look so wretchedly ill, so utterly exhausted and worn out; and I remember that, more than once, I covered my face with the paper that he might not see the tear which I could not prevent from trickling down my cheek. After one of these painful reveries, suddenly my eye fell upon a paragraph in the paper which at once absorbed all my attention and engrossed all my energies. I read it through two or three times, in a wondering kind of a way, before I understood its full bearing and import; but, at last, I took it all in, and with a loud cry I let the paper fall from my hand. The paragraph which caught my eye was to this effect:—" We regret to learn through the foreign papers that a boat accident, attended with melancholy results, occurred some days ago in the Mediterranean. Mr. Rupert Percy, the eldest son and heir of Sir Percy Percy, of Percy Grange, has been abroad for some time. A few days ago he engaged a pleasure boat for a short cruise on the Mediterranean. The vessel had not been at sea more than a few hours when she was caught in a sudden squall, and melancholy to relate, all on board were lost. One of the oldest families in the North has thus been plunged into grief and mourning. We understand that the unfortunate gentleman was a youth of brilliant talents and of great promise; and his sad fate is to be the more deplored as it is stated that the present heir to the ancient title and the vast estates of Percy Grange some years ago seceded from the church of his baptism to the Church of Rome."

Eustace was startled by my cry, and he ran hastily over to my side, thinking that I had been taken ill. After a few hurried words of preparation, I took up the paper and showed him the paragraph which contained an announcement of such immense importance to him, an importance which could scarcely be over-estimated, and which, perhaps, we hardly realized all at once. I saw at a glance, however, how wonderfully the prospects of my friend were changed, and my heart glowed with honest exultation at the thought. Now, indeed, Sir Percy might still harden his heart against his child, still keep him in straitened circumstances as long as he lived; but his power to injure must pass with his life. He could not alienate a single acre of his vast estates. The only thought that gave me any pain, and it shot through me with a sudden pang even in this moment, was the fear that Eustace, who had long looked so worn out and broken down, might never live to take possession of the vast domain to which he was now the undisputed heir. But I determined at the same moment, in my inmost heart, that he *should* now change his manner of life, that he *should* cherish and take care of that health which was now precious to so many besides himself, that he *should* watch over that life which might be of such service to God and holy church; and I knew well enough that this last argument was one by which I could bring him round to my purposes, by which I could cause him to do many things from which, on any other ground, he would have turned away with indifference or contempt. Hence, as I thought of all these and a thousand other things which rushed tumultuously through my brain, my heart, as I have just said, glowed with honest exultation. Not that I rejoiced at the sudden and sad death of poor Rupert Percy—God forbid. But, knowing him as I had known him—watching him through all his boyhood's years, as I had watched him—marking all the labours and the wearing cares of these later times, as I had marked them—admiring with loving reverence his heroic practice of Christian virtue, as I had admired and reverenced it—with my consciousness of those noble qualities which would make him such a Christian and a Catholic gentleman—knowing as I knew how the widow and the orphan would laud his name, how that name would be in benediction amongst the blessed poor of God—cherishing him as I cherished him, and loving him as I loved him,—considering how the light had come at the very moment when the clouds were darkest, and the future seemed most hopeless—I should have been less than a man if, in that moment of sudden triumph I had not for an instant clasped him to my heart, that I might weep hot tears of joyful exultation upon his breast, tears that were forced from me by my grateful thankfulness for the glorious fortune which had fallen upon one who was so infinitely worthy of it, one who would bear his triumphs even as he had borne his sorrows, one who had been carried through a sea of suffering to a haven of tranquillity and rest, one who was surely none the less dearly loved and prized by me because the first words which fell from him in that trying moment were the expression of a piteous cry, " Rupert—my poor brother—Rupert! God knows I never thought or wished for this. Rupert —my brother—oh, my brother, Rupert!"

Within an hour or two of this, and before we had recovered from the state of perturbation into which we had been thrown by this intelligence, we were destined to receive a greater and still more startling shock. In the course of the forenoon a telegraphic message, as it was called in those days, was handed to Eustace. It was from the legal adviser of the family, and was very brief, containing merely the following words: " Sir Percy is very ill; come without delay." We saw at once that this was a summons which admitted of no procrastination, although it was impossible to make out from its terms whether it had been sent at Sir Percy's request, or without his knowledge. Poor Eustace clung to the former supposition, and cherished the pleasing hope that the unforgiving heart had relented at last. As he pressed me earnestly to accompany him on this sad journey, I made the necessary preparations, and we started that same evening.

The railway to York had been opened a short time previous to this, and we travelled by the night train, arriving at York next morning. Thence we journeyed, as fast as four horses could carry us, to Percy Grange. During the whole journey, Eustace, naturally enough, was in pitiable agitation and distress of mind. The intelligence of his father's illness following so soon on that of his brother's death, had been almost too much for him, and I felt deeply thankful that I had accompanied him. The only thought which brought a ray of comfort to him was the idea that his father had sent for him. " You know, Ambrose," he said to me I think at least fifty times during the journey, " you know if we were only reconciled—if I could only hear one word of loving pardon from his lips,—I think that I could almost bear the rest." That loving word—I cannot call it of pardon where there was nothing to forgive—he was never destined to hear, but he never ceased to yearn the less deeply, the less ardently for it, on that account.

I did my best to console him and bring comfort to his troubled soul, as we journeyed on, and about mid-day we arrived at Percy Grange. The carriage had scarcely stopped ere Mr. Rogers, the solicitor of the family, who had sent the message to Eustace, opened the door to receive us. In the low bow with which he bent to my friend it was plain to me that he had heard of Rupert's death, and that he was conscious, and wished to express his consciousness, of the fact that he was receiving the future master of Percy Grange. He led us in, and in a few seconds we were in possession of the state of the case. The first information which Sir Percy had received of the death of his eldest son had been quite sudden, and through the medium of the newspaper in which we, too, had seen the intelligence. There were visitors at the Grange at the time, and they were seated at breakfast, Sir Percy sitting at the head of the table. All at once the paper which he held, and which he had been reading, fell from his hands. Then they noticed what seemed to be a fearful spasm, contracting and distorting the features of his face. Before it had passed away he rose from his seat, threw his arms wildly above his head, and, in an instant more, with a loud cry fell heavily on the floor. When they raised him they found him writhing in all the terrible contortions of a very serious fit. They carried him to his bed, and summoned medical aid. After a while the doctors succeeded in reducing the more violent symptoms of his attack; but, although still alive, he had never spoken, nor shown the slightest sign of consciousness since the moment he had fallen down, a broken and a shattered wreck, upon the floor of his stately home.

Such was the story which the lawyer told us in a few brief dry words. "I was staying in the house at the time," he went on to say, addressing his words deferentially to Eustace, "and I deemed it my duty to send for you at once. After Sir Percy had been removed, I took up the paper which had dropped from his hands, and my eyes at once fell upon the paragraph containing the melancholy intelligence of the death of poor Mr. Rupert. Of course this gave us a clue to his sudden attack. I have taken upon myself the responsibility of sending for you, sir, because I deem it of the last importance that you should be upon the spot, in order to be ready to meet any contingency which may arise. In the melancholy circumstances in which we are placed," he went on, with more feeling than I could have expected from him, "I will not pretend to offer you my congratulations on the happy change in your fortunes. I will merely remind you that you are now the undoubted heir to every acre of the Percy estates." He bowed a little lower as he spoke, and then continued: "But I also deem it my duty to remind you that there is, too, a very large amount of personal and valuable property to be disposed of. How Sir Percy might have disposed of this property I will not presume to say. All that I will say is that he has *not* disposed of it, inasmuch as I had come hither at his request in order to draw up his will; and this was to have been done the very day on which he was stricken down. Pardon me if I pain you, Mr. Eustace, with these sad details," he added, as poor Eustace turned away his head and cried aloud in uncontrollable agony; " but it is my duty to do so, although I do assure you it is a very painful duty. I have not served this noble and this honoured family for nearly sixty years without having acquired a deep interest in its fortunes and its welfare; and its members must ever be objects of deep but respectful solicitude to me. Sir Percy may be spared to us," he continued. " God grant that it may be so, but it is by far the most painful part of my duty to have to inform you," laying his hand respectfully on Eustace's shoulder, " that the doctors give but the very slightest hopes of his recovery. They add that he will probably pass away without having regained consciousness. Should he do so, I need not remind you how large a portion of this personal property will be yours by every right and title. Far be it from me to impute unworthy motives, or to insinuate that unfair advantages may be taken," he went on, his brow contracting ever so little, " but this I do say," he added, earnestly, " that every precaution must be taken that a dying man is not tampered with. If it shall please God to restore his senses, for ever so brief a space, to Sir Percy, let him by all means dispose of his property as he may wish. No man can question his right to do so. If it shall happen otherwise, it is my duty, and it is yours, sir, a thousand times more, to see that he is not tampered with. Since he was stricken down yesterday morning, I have never left his side till this moment; although I have been but an unwelcome guest," he added, thus hinting, as I understood plainly enough, his suspicions of my Lady. " But I have done my duty. That duty, sir, I now resign into your hands, assuring you that you may rely, to the full, upon any assistance or advice which I can give you in these very painful and trying circumstances."

The old man who had served the family until its interests were, no doubt, as dear to him as his own, brushed away a tear from his eye with the back of his hand as he concluded; whilst Eustace, who had listened with a weary and distracted look to his story, turned away his head, and laying his face upon the table once more, wept and cried aloud in all the vehemence of that grief which refuses to be comforted; of that grief which wrings such short, fierce sobs out of the heart of a man alone; of that grief whose every cry is a groan, whose every sigh seems as if it would burst in twain the heaving breast from which it forces its way.

When Eustace had become somewhat composed, the lawyer led us up to Sir Percy's room. As we passed suddenly from the light of day into the gloom and obscurity of the darkened chamber where the sick man lay, it was a few moments before I could take in the leading features of the scene which met my view. At last my eyes became accustomed to the gloom, and I looked around me. The rich curtains of the bed were only partially drawn, and by the light of the shaded lamp, which stood upon a table at a little distance, I recognized the face of the dying man. He lay upon his bed, pale and motionless, giving no sign of life, except the heavy breathing which sounded with painful distinctness through the unnatural quiet of the sick room. But yesterday morning, and he had sat at the head of his table as handsome and as stately-looking a gentleman as you would have seen in all England, and, now, he lay upon his bed a miserable and a shattered wreck, so utterly changed and beaten out of shape, that I, well as I knew him, could scarcely recognize him. He was certainly the first object to which I turned my eyes on entering the room, but my attention was almost simultaneously directed to my Lady. She sat at the top of the bed, with one of her arms resting on the pillow where the head of the sick man lay, whilst with the other she clasped her son, who was now a very handsome boy of some eleven years of age, closely to her side. She never moved as we entered, neither did she speak. She only withdrew her eyes for an instant from the face of the dying man, and glared at us with a fierce and angry stare. I have said that she *glared* at us, for I do not know any other word which would, in any measure, express the terrible character of the look which she cast upon us. Her long, black hair was hanging in disordered masses about her face, which was as beautiful as ever, although with a beauty that had something very fearful and appalling in it. Her features were as rigid as marble, whilst the deadly pallor of her countenance gave an unnatural lustre to her eyes, which seemed to burn in her head like two living fires. She cast but one glance upon us as we entered the room, but there was a world of fierce impatience at our presence, a world of baffled hopes and bitter disappointment, expressed in that one glance. And, yet, it was wonderful, nay, it was even touching, to see how the fierce glance softened as she turned away from us with an angry frown, and once more cast her eyes upon the face of the dying man; once more drew her boy, for whose sake, perhaps, she had sinned so deeply, closer to her side. When Eustace went over to her and held out his hand, she took no more notice of him than if he had been a thousand miles away; but when he stooped down and drew the weeping boy tenderly to his breast, and kissed him on his brow, she did not attempt to prevent him. To all appearance her whole being was absorbed in the great blow, in the crushing sorrow which had fallen so suddenly upon her; and if our entrance had, for an instant, turned her thoughts into another and more angry channel, they were again immediately concentrated upon her own overwhelming grief, her own bitter disappointment, and, it may have been, her own fierce despair, the moment she turned her looks once more to the face of the dying man. If she had played a double part—if she had hardened the heart of the broken, shattered man who lay before her eyes against his son, that she might thus gain possession of his wealth for herself and for her own boy, she had played a very wicked and a very treacherous game. As every breath which rose with laboured effort from his breast—as every drop of sweat which rolled along his clammy face—as every fleeting minute which bore him nearer to that eternity to which he was hastening, proclaimed to her that the stake, for which she had played such a deep and fearful game, was slipping more and more surely from her grasp, what wonder if the light grew more and more terrible in her eye, what wonder if the features of her face grew more and more rigid in their stern despair, what wonder if she turned aside in angry impatience from all the world beside, that she might bend her burning gaze upon the face of the dying man, that she might draw her innocent child with such a frantic earnestness to her guilty breast!

We had arrived at Percy Grange on Wednesday afternoon, and he remained in the same condition, without any perceptible change, until Saturday night. During all this time Eustace and my Lady never left him except for a few brief moments. They sat at the head of his bed, one on each side, gazing with solemn looks upon his paling face, watching with eager earnestness for the slightest indication of returning consciousness. Whilst I am quite sure that there was no other wish in the heart of Eustace except that his father might not pass away without having breathed the one word of love, of peace, of reconciliation, for which the heart of his son did so yearn and crave, I have little doubt that my Lady waited and watched with far other motives. I do not mean to say that she did not love her husband. I am sure that she did, that she loved him deeply and ardently, loved him with a fierce and passionate vehemence which is only felt by natures such as hers. But, one five minutes of restored consciousness to Sir Percy might be of such overwhelming importance to her; might have such an influence on the stake for which she had played, and perhaps sinned, so deeply; might make such a change in her future fortunes and those of her son, that I am certain I do her no injustice when I say that the motives which filled her breast, as she sat night and day watching with such straining eagerness for those few minutes of returning reason and of sense, which seemed as if they would never come, were of a very different kind from those which stirred in the breast of Eustace.

At all events, whatever their motives might be, they sat and watched through all those weary days and nights, whilst he, who was the object of so much anxious care, went down step by step, slowly but surely, to the silent grave. I have remarked that I was very thankful that I had accompanied Eustace on this sad journey. I repeat what I have already said, as no one but myself and God can ever know how much he stood in need of the help and assistance, which I am grateful to be able to remember, that it was in my power to afford him during these trying days. Without that help and assistance, such as it was—without his own lively faith and perfect conformity to the adorable will of God, which so strengthened and sustained his fainting soul, I think, weak and enfeebled as he already was, that he would have sunk under the trial.

On Saturday night he was so utterly exhausted and worn out that, after many urgent entreaties, he allowed me to take his place by his father's bed for two or three hours. He would not, however, consent to leave the room, but merely stretched himself upon a sofa in a distant part of the apartment, which was very large. As I took my place, my Lady raised her eyes for one instant, and gazed at me with that fierce look of hers, but that was all. Not a sound disturbed the stillness of the room, except the heavy breathing of the suffering man, as I sat watching the terrible expression that seemed each instant to settle more and more deeply into every line of my Lady's beautiful face, till I almost grew afraid to gaze at it, till my very blood seemed to freeze within my veins. I cannot tell exactly when it happened, but, sometime towards midnight, worn out with watching I had fallen off into a doze. Suddenly, I awoke with a great start, and, in that same instant, I became conscious that something extraordinary was taking place on the other side of the bed. I was sitting in the heavy shadow of the curtain, but I peered cautiously round the edge of it. To my intense astonishment, I saw that the eyes of the dying man were open, I saw that he was conscious. I saw that my Lady was speaking to him in a low tone of voice, but with a vehemence which shook her whole frame till she could scarcely stand. By the fragments of the words which I caught, I knew that she was striving to awaken him to still greater consciousness. With all her ambitious designs, all her hopes and fears concentrated in terrible energy upon that moment which must, of necessity, be of such intense interest to her, I gathered that she was urging him to endeavour to sign a deed, which she held ready in her hand, and which I had little doubt she would, in an instant more, if she succeeded in her purpose

call upon me and Eustace to witness. But I
marked that he gave no sign. As my Lady,
holding her boy before his eyes, urged him
with burning words, I marked a troubled expression pass across his face. I saw him look
wearily around the room, and, then, I rose softly
and went over and laid my arm upon the shoulder
of Eustace. He sprung to his feet in an instant,
and, as I pointed to the bed, he seemed to understand it all. He ran over with hurried steps, and
threw himself upon his knees, and caught his
father's hand. When the dying man saw who it
was, a faint smile passed for an instant across his
face; a smile which told with unutterable eloquence the tale which my poor friend had so
longed and yearned to hear; a smile which spoke
of the love of years gone by; a smile which,
whilst with a meaning that none might misunderstand, it craved for pardon for the past, spoke
above all, in that last flickering moment of his life,
of nought but love, and peace, and reconciliation
with his child. As Eustace rose from his knees,
and, in the shadow of the great change that was
upon him, kissed him reverently upon the brow,
he opened his eyes once more, and, once more
looked lovingly upon them all—upon her, and upon
Eustace, and upon his little boy—with a look that
seemed to ask of them to love each other for his
sake—with a look which seemed to say that all
the shadows of the past had cleared at last—with

a look which seemed to say that he left his wife and his little boy, his vast estates and his honoured name, with confidence in the keeping of the son from whom he had been so long estranged, the son whose eyes reflected back, with such a depth of earnest truth, his own last longing look of love, as, gently drifting from the troubled ocean of his life, he passed away beyond the everlasting shores.

* * * * * * *

A few days more, and the family vault in the gray, old churchyard, where so many of his fathers slept, was opened to receive another tenant. A few days more, and Sir Percy Percy was laid by the side of that long line of noble ancestors, whose name he had borne, and whose honour and renown he had so highly prized. A few days more, and the bells were clanging out with merry peal, to spread the tidings far and wide, through all the country round, that Sir Eustace lived and ruled at Percy Grange, the honoured lord and master of its vast domain.

CHAPTER XVII.

CONCLUSION.

Turn we, at last, from the stormy ocean, the seething waves, and the howling winds, amid which our course has lain so long, to where the sunlights twinkle with a gentle ray upon the rippling bosom of the calm and placid sea. Wave after wave has swept us on our way, drifting us ever nearer and nearer to those everlasting shores whose outline seems to be already breaking on our sight. Another wave or two, and the ocean of life, with its storms as with its calms, will be for us but a thing of the past, a thing to be forgotten and swallowed up in the immensity of the great *evermore* into which we shall have been launched.

Sitting in my chair, that I may write the closing pages of this simple narrative, and looking back from the shelter of the haven at which I have nearly arrived, upon the ocean of my life, my heart begins to swell with grateful thankfulness to Him whose favouring hand has helped me on my way with such abundant succour, with a succour which has ever been the greatest when my need was sorest; whose face has smiled with such cheering hope upon me in my struggles with the stormy waves. I have been a very happy and a very favoured man. I have not proposed to myself to tell much of my own story in this book. It has been my happy lot to minister to God's children through many passing years; my happy lot to lead many wanderers to His feet; my happy lot to labour for the glory of His holy name, and, everywhere, the gracious condescension which called me has crowned my poor efforts with an abundant and an overflowing blessing. For some season it was a great trouble to me that the mother, who was so dear to me on many titles, did not think as I thought, nor pray as I prayed, but it pleased my Master, in His own good time, to remove this affliction from me; and she, whose life had been so blameless, even whilst a wanderer outside the saving fold, ran rapidly in the way of holy perfection when God had enlarged her heart, and brought her into His Church; that, after edifying every one with whom she came in contact during her life, she might die the death of a saint, leaving a memory to be held in benediction by all who knew her, a memory to be for ever shrined in the purest and the best affections of the son whose hand pens, with a love which few may guess, this simple tribute to the memory of one who is as dear to him to-day as when he knelt, long, long years ago, in childish and in loving innocence at that mother's feet.

I have been a happy man, too, on many other grounds. I think I need scarcely tell you, gentle reader, what a joy it was to me to see Sir Eustace Percy installed, without dispute, in all his rights as lord and master of the ancient title and the vast domains of Percy Grange. I think I need scarcely tell you of the pride with which I saw him act with a justice and a liberality, which, although they were no more than I expected from him, I may truly call profuse, towards his father's widow and his half brother; a liberality which, although, unfortunately thrown away upon her, had the effect of joining the two brothers in a bond of the closest affection and love. I think I need scarcely tell you of the gratification with which I saw him united in due time to one who was worthy of him in every point of view, one who has shared with him in all his good works, and been foremost in carrying out his designs for the advantage of the poor, for the promotion of the holy Catholic Faith. They have passed through life doing good to all; with a keen appreciation of the duties which are imposed upon them by their exalted station; with a never-flagging diligence in the discharge of those duties towards God and towards their fellow men; exhibiting to the world the beautiful and the sublime picture of a Christian and a Catholic gentleman and his wife. As I walk through their domain, and see, at a little distance, the spire of the stately church which their grateful munificence has raised to the glory of God; as I listen to the blessings which greet the mention of their names in every cottage on their estate which I chance to enter; as I think how the prayers of the widow and orphan are ever rising for them to the throne of God, it is little wonder if my heart grows full, even to overflowing, with gratitude to God, with admiration and with love for them. I can scarcely trust myself to speak of all their goodness, all their love, all their tender solicitude for me, and all my little wants. Their eldest boy bears my name. He is their hope and their pride. He is my hope and my pride, too. He has his father's face, and his father's form, and his father's virtues are budding forth afresh in him. I have advanced so far on the journey of my life that I am now obliged to give myself a good deal of rest, and it would be an offence, which they would never pardon, were I to take that rest elsewhere than at Percy Grange. Often and often he gathers his children about his feet, and tells them what he calls the story of his life, only I can scarcely recognize it. As he speaks of the days gone by—as he tells them, whilst the tears are coursing down his noble face, that he owes his life and all that he has to the loving care and the generous help of a faithful friend—as he lifts his hand and points to me, what can I do but rise in confusion from my seat, and hurry over, that I may place my finger on his lips. As I see his children kneeling at my feet—as I feel his hand in mine—as I look once more into those eyes, whose glance is as pure and true as ever it was in the days of old—what wonder if I am fain to turn away my head, what wonder if the words of benediction on him and his, which are trembling on my lips, pass away from me and leave me speechless with gratitude and love; leave me with nothing but my tears, with nothing but the aspirations of my heart to God for those whom, in very truth, I love more dearly than all the world besides, but whom, I trust, I do not love more than it is fitting for me to do!

And, thus, we are drifting away, calmly and gently, from the ocean of our life, to our everlasting rest. Did I say too much when I said that the sunlights were beaming with a gentle ray upon the rippling bosom of the calm and placid sea. I am fain to believe that the light which has never been wanting is shining down upon me as I pen these parting words. It shines upon the Past, with all its struggles and its toils. It shines upon the Present, with all its benedictions and its hopes. With its brightest and its most unclouded radiance, it shines upon the Future which grows nearer every day, that Future which, please God, shall crown for evermore the Present and the Past.

THE END.

www.ingramcontent.com/pod-product-compliance
Lightning Source LLC
Chambersburg PA
CBHW021204230426
43667CB00006B/547